Striking First

THE UNIVERSITY CENTER
FOR HUMAN VALUES SERIES

STEPHEN MACEDO, EDITOR

Multiculturalism and "The Politics of Recognition"
by Charles Taylor

*A Matter of Interpretation: Federal
Courts and the Law*
by Antonin Scalia

Freedom of Association
edited by Amy Gutmann

Work and Welfare
by Robert M. Solow

The Lives of Animals
by J. M. Coetzee

*Truth v. Justice: The Morality
of Truth Commissions*
edited by Robert I. Rotberg and Dennis Thompson

Goodness and Advice
by Judith Jarvis Thomson

Human Rights as Politics and Idolatry
by Michael Ignatieff

Democracy, Culture and the Voice of Poetry
by Robert Pinsky

Primates and Philosophers: How Morality Evolved
by Frans de Waal

*Striking First: Preemption and Prevention
in International Conflict*
by Michael W. Doyle

STRIKING FIRST

PREEMPTION AND PREVENTION IN INTERNATIONAL CONFLICT

MICHAEL W. DOYLE

EDITED AND INTRODUCED BY
STEPHEN MACEDO

WITH COMMENTARY BY
HAROLD HONGJU KOH • RICHARD TUCK •
JEFF McMAHAN

PRINCETON UNIVERSITY PRESS   PRINCETON AND OXFORD

Copyright © 2008 by Princeton University Press

Published by Princeton University Press,
41 William Street, Princeton, New Jersey 08540
In the United Kingdom: Princeton University Press,
6 Oxford Street, Woodstock, Oxfordshire OX20 1TW
All Rights Reserved

Library of Congress Cataloging-in-Publication Data
Doyle, Michael W., 1948–
Striking first : preemption and prevention in international
conflict / Michael W. Doyle ; edited and introduced by
Stephen Macedo ; with commentary by Harold Hongju Koh,
Richard Tuck, Jeff McMahan.
    p.   cm.
Includes index.
ISBN 978-0-691-13658-5 (hbk. : alk. paper) 1. Intervention
(International law) 2. Sanctions (International law) 3. Preemptive
attack (Military science) 4. War (International law)—
Philosophy. 5. National security—United States.
I. Macedo, Stephen, 1957– II. Title.
KZ6368.D69 2008
341.5'8—dc22
                    2007043299

British Library Cataloging-in-Publication Data is available

This book has been composed in Sabon with Trajan display type

Printed on acid-free paper ∞

press.princeton.edu

Printed in the United States of America

1   3   5   7   9   10   8   6   4   2

CONTENTS

❖

CONTENTS

ACKNOWLEDGMENTS

MICHAEL W. DOYLE

N o one could be more fortunate than I have been in having had Jeff McMahan, Ruth Wedgwood, Harold Koh, and Richard Tuck as commentators. The four have made pathbreaking contributions to international ethics, law, and political theory, and specifically to the topic of preventive self-defense. Each read the drafts of the lectures with care, shared their opinions with candor, and made these essays before you much better than they would have been without their generous commentary.[1] I am thoroughly grateful that this "Dream Team" agreed to share their thoughts with me and with the lively audience that heard the lectures in November 2006, at Princeton.

[1] All four commentators provided extensive and incisive commentary on the lectures. Ruth Wedgwood's comments focused more on the details, less on the broad contours, and offered numerous suggestions, many adopted in the revised text printed here. She chose not to publish them, but they were helpful to me.

ACKNOWLEDGMENTS

These lectures also benefited from the insights I gained from the two seminars, two lunches, and two dinners organized by Professor Kim Scheppele, and reflect the suggestions she shared based on her own important work on the political and legal dangers being generated abroad by the war on terrorism. The welcome completion of the lengthy process from Professor Stephen Macedo's invitation, to the lectures, and now to the book before you reflects the dedicated shepherding of Jan Logan of the University Center for Human Values and Chuck Myers of Princeton Press. This book also reflects the careful copyediting of Lauren Lepow. The two and a half days I spent delivering the lectures and responding in the seminars were the single most insightful academic experience I have had.

I also thank Makael Burrell and Alexandra Newton for proofing; Lars Christie, Asrat Tefayesus, and Keren Tenenbaum for excellent research assistance; and Geoffrey Carlson, of Columbia Law School, for many helpful suggestions. Dan Noble, of Yale Law School, provided both research assistance and painstaking editorial advice that saved me from many mistakes. Dan also traveled to Princeton to hear the results of our joint labors. Bruce Ackerman, Michael Barnett, Allan Erbsen, Hal Feiveson, Amy Gutmann, Oona Hathaway, Sam Issacharoff, Paul Kahn, Robert Keohane, Steve Macedo, Kal Raustiala, David Schizer, Peter Schuck, Ian Shapiro, Michael Smith, and Michael Walzer made many insightful suggestions, all of which I found useful in revising the lectures. Versions of these lectures were presented to the members of my Anticipatory Self Defense seminar at Columbia Law School and my Use of Force seminar at Yale Law School. I also shared early versions at the University of Minnesota, Ohio State University's Mershon Center, and Yale Law School's faculty seminar. I benefited from helpful discussions at all these events and in particular suggestions from T. Chhabra, Medha Devanagondi, Kristen Eichensehr, Brian Lee, and Kim Sullivan. I am grateful for the support of a Guggenheim Fellowship and a continuing grant from The Christian Johnson Endeavor Foundation.

INTRODUCTION

Stephen Macedo

Should a responsible government try to deter a potential foe, or should it strike first—that is, preventively—to spare itself from a blow that the other seems to intend, has delivered before, and could again deliver? Is it safer to wait and threaten punishment than to throw the first punch? Or is it wiser to strike now, before the risks increase, even though that means taking the chance that the danger might not materialize?

These are among the questions raised by Michael W. Doyle's timely and important essays, originally presented as Tanner Lectures on Human Values, delivered at Princeton University in November 2006. Doyle addresses not only the underlying moral question of the conditions under which preventive war is justified, but also the complex practical question of how, if at all, international law should be refashioned in the current era of terrorist networks and heightened insecurity to accommodate resorts to preventive war—or anticipatory self-defense.

At stake are some of the greatest foreign and defense policy controversies of our time. The United Nations has declared that "[s]tates shall refrain in their international relations from the threat or use of force against the territorial integrity or political independence of any State."[1] But the "Bush Doctrine," announced in the National Security Strategy document of 2002, said that in the face of terrorist networks supported by hostile states, the United States would not "remain idle while dangers gather," but rather would seek to "pre-empt emerging threats."[2] Henceforth, the United States was prepared to attack another state in the absence of evidence of an impending attack, and without the authorization of the Security Council, as required by Article 39 of the UN Charter.[3]

[1] Declaration on Principles of International Law Concerning Friendly Relations and Co-operation among States in accordance with the Charter of the United Nations, G.A. res. 2625, Annex, 25 UN GAOR, Supp. (No. 28), U.N. Doc. A/5217 at 121 (1970).

[2] *The National Security Strategy of the United States of America,* Washington, D.C., September 2002 (available online, http://www.whitehouse.gov/nsc/nss.html), 15.

[3] Article 39 reads, "The Security Council shall determine the existence of any threat to the peace, breach of the peace, or act of aggression and shall make recommendations, or decide what measures shall be taken in accordance with Articles 41 and 42, to maintain or restore international peace and security."

This marked a departure from international law and presaged the invasion of Iraq in 2003.

Doyle is uniquely well-qualified to address both the moral and legal questions surrounding preventive war. He is a renowned scholar of empire, peace, war, and international law, whose work has been widely influential among political philosophers as well as students and practitioners of international relations. But Doyle is not only a leading scholar; he has also served as assistant secretary-general of the United Nations and special adviser to United Nations Secretary-General Kofi Annan, with special responsibilities for strategic planning and relations with Washington. Michael Doyle is joined in this volume by three exceptionally well-qualified commentators who contest some of his central claims.

The reigning orthodoxy under international law—or under what Michael Walzer calls the "legalist paradigm"—is that a resort to war is permissible only under two narrow and carefully defined conditions.[4] The first and clearest case of just war is defensive: to defend against an unjust attacker and to secure the conditions of peace. The country that is attacked and others may join in the defensive war in order to repel, and perhaps also to punish, an unjust attacker.[5]

Beyond defensive war, international law and the dominant strand of just war theory allow for one additional narrow category of just war: *preemptive war* in response

[4] *Just and Unjust Wars: A Moral Argument with Historical Illustrations,* 3rd ed. (New York: Basic, 2000), 75.

[5] See the discussion in Jeff McMahan's essay, below.

to a threat of attack that is not only overwhelming but also so imminent as to allow no time for deliberation and no choice of means.[6] A classic example of justified preemptive war—at least in the judgment of many commentators—occurred when tiny Israel, ringed by hostile neighbors, faced an Egyptian army massed on its borders in 1967 and, instead of waiting, struck first.

If these two sorts of cases exhaust the category of "just war," then the Bush Doctrine of *prevention*—misleadingly labeled as "preemption"—cannot be justified. According to this doctrine, the United States may undertake "anticipatory action" against "emerging threats": prevention is triggered by gathering threats that are neither as imminent nor as overwhelming as the threat faced by Israel in 1967, when it feared being overrun by hostile invading armies. This is especially so if we take seriously the "one percent doctrine" that has been associated with Vice President Richard Cheney, according to which even a 1 percent chance of terrorists' coming into possession of a weapon of mass destruction is too great a chance and should be treated as a certainty.[7] The Bush

---

[6] Richard Tuck emphasizes that there are contending strands of thinking about just causes of war, with the Scholastic tradition defending the narrow account described here. See Tuck's essay below, and also Walzer, *Just and Unjust Wars*, 77–78.

[7] Ron Suskind, *The One Percent Doctrine: Deep Inside America's Pursuit of Its Enemies since 9/11* (New York: Simon & Schuster, 2006). In Suskind's words, "if there was even a 1 percent chance of terrorists getting a weapon of mass destruction—and there has been a small probability of such an occurrence for some time—the United States must now act as if it were a certainty."

Doctrine appears to be expansive and flexible, whereas the traditional view is supposed to be narrow and restrictive. In addition, whereas international law insists on Security Council authorization, U.S. policy evidently contemplates action that is unilateral or undertaken by ad hoc "coalitions of the willing."

Some critics of the Bush administration, and others, will argue that widening the doctrine of preventive war is too dangerous to be contemplated or encouraged. In an unstable international environment leaders of militarily powerful states are apt to be all too ready to look abroad for growing threats. This is perhaps especially so in democratic societies, in which citizens and the media are apt to magnify fears and insecurities, and to minimize the costs inflicted on distant others by military actions. Moreover, amidst the great differences over values and perceptions that mark the international arena, common standards will be lacking for assessing the reasonableness of judgments based on intelligence sources and extrapolations from historical patterns. To license in advance unilateral preventive war is to create too great a danger that the most powerful countries, and in particular the United States with its vast military machine, will imagine and act against perceived threats where there are none. As the old saying has it (more or less), if you have a really excellent hammer, everything is liable to look like a nail.

Michael Doyle argues that the traditional international law orthodoxy is unrealistic and excessively constraining given the conditions that now confront world leaders, including the new threats posed by nonstate actors such as terrorist networks and the states that support them. The inherited legalist orthodoxy offers too little to nations facing a variety of threats, both immediate and gathering (indeed, Doyle makes clear that the traditional legalist principles of just war did not altogether rule against preventive uses of force).[8] At the same time, he also argues that the Bush Doctrine offers too broad and unstructured a warrant for the use of force: too little by way of clear and justifiable standards to guide the resort to preventive war in the face of gathering threats.

The task that Doyle has set for himself in these essays is no less than to articulate the conditions under which preventive war is justified, and to specify workable and useful criteria that ought to be recognized by the international community to guide, constrain, and assess the resort to preventive war. Doyle treads a delicate course. He aims to strengthen international law by, first, broadening it to encompass a ground for war making that has the admitted potential for being dangerously expansive, but, second, to assert standards that, if also recognized in international law, can improve political deliberation about decisions to make war on anticipatory or preventive grounds.

These two essays, the comments that follow, and Doyle's response provide a window on central questions of war and peace. They also require us to consider how international law and international institutions can

[8] Walzer also argues that the traditional legalist paradigm, associated with Daniel Webster and the *Caroline* doctrine, strictly interpreted is overly restrictive; see *Just and Unjust Wars*, 76–79.

guide political deliberation and constrain state behavior
with respect to the gravest decisions confronting political leaders.

Doyle's four standards are spelled out in his second
essay. They encompass criteria related to the lethality
and likelihood of the gathering threat, and the legitimacy
(reasonableness and proportionality) of the contemplated response. Consistent with his desire to strengthen
international law and institutions, and his confidence in
their efficacy, he insists that another basic requirement
for countries contemplating a resort to preventive war is
that they must make their case to international institutions, especially the UN Security Council. The resort to
multilateral authorization in an international forum
should, Doyle hopes, help temper the danger that risks,
when assessed from a purely national standpoint, will
be exaggerated. An international forum like the Security
Council may be less prone to the sorts of panics and un-
critical "groupthink" that occur domestically when
countries feel threatened and patriotic fervor is inflamed.

But what is to be done when multilateral forums such
as the Security Council fail to behave reasonably and responsibly? The Security Council has some admirable
characteristics as compared with national decision making; at any given time it will include diplomatic representatives of a broad array of the world's states. But the
Security Council—and every other available procedural
mechanism—is by no means sufficiently reliable to be
accorded the authority to decide for states. Arbitrari-
ness and error are ever-present possibilities, in part be-

cause of the veto power possessed by the permanent members. NATO's bombing campaign to force Slobodan Milošević to withdraw his forces from Kosovo bypassed the United Nations on account of a threatened Russian veto. And of course, the UN lacks its own enforcement mechanisms.

Doyle allows that there must be an option for preventive actions that are unsanctioned by the UN Security Council and other multilateral bodies; history shows that preventive wars will occur, and sometimes with good reason. His four conditions are not rigid "necessary and sufficient conditions," but rather justificatory factors or standards to be applied as criteria for justification and assessment. It also needs to be emphasized that these justificatory standards aim not only to constrain decision making, but to improve it, regarded from both domestic and international standpoints. Nations inflamed by anger and fears in the wake of a terrorist or military attack—like the United States in the wake of 9/11—may, for example, discount the value *to themselves* of multilateral forums. They may discount the value of securing multilateral cooperation, and register only frustration at the "checks and balances" provided by the need to convince an audience not directly affected by an attack. But in fact, as in the case of domestic constitutional hurdles furnished by mechanisms such as judicial review and bicameralism, multilateral institutions can improve domestic decision making by increasing opportunities for cool reflection.[9] Doyle's standards,

---

[9] For reflections along these lines, see Stephen Holmes, *The Mata-*

therefore, speak not only to those who would constrain states in the name of transnational values and interests, but to those who would improve domestic decision making regarded solely from a domestic viewpoint.

Doyle's argument is philosophically subtle, and deeply informed by his long study of international conflicts as well as his practical experience. His recommendations on how international law should be adapted to accommodate and guide resorts to preventive war deserve to be taken seriously. Not everyone will be convinced, and this volume includes short critical essays by three eminent commentators who express significant reservations about aspects of Doyle's argument.

Dean Harold Hongju Koh applauds Michael Doyle's efforts to articulate standards to channel and guide exercises of anticipatory force that are sanctioned multilaterally. He denies, however, that the international community should ever acknowledge standards that allow for the prior justification of *unilateral* anticipatory or preventive military action. It is one thing to allow states or coalitions of states to bypass institutions like the UN Security Council for the sake of *humanitarian* interventions. The incentive for states to intervene on humanitarian grounds is typically limited, and the forces needed to

---

dor's Cape: America's Reckless Response to Terror (Cambridge: Cambridge University Press, 2007); and also Robert O. Keohane, Stephen Macedo, and Andrew Moravcsik, "Democracy-Enhancing Multilateralism," working paper, Institute for International Law and Justice, New York University School of Law, 2007, available on line at http://www.iilj.org/working%20papers/2007-4KMMGA.htm.

put a stop to humanitarian crises, Koh argues, can be estimated and agreed upon. But in cases where nations have been attacked and are contemplating a military response—like that of the post-9/11 United States—Koh argues that criteria of the sort that Doyle has articulated, including factors such as likelihood and proportionality—are simply too subjective, flexible, and open to self-serving interpretation. Democratic leaders in particular may have great incentive to regard even a small risk as too great a risk. Electoral incentives seem to favor shows of massive strength and a determination to defend the "homeland" even against speculative threats, and even in the face of great costs imposed on nonnationals. Koh argues that Doyle's four standards are unlikely to constrain leaders of states that feel threatened.

Koh argues for the value of maintaining a standing categorical prohibition on *unilateral* preventive or anticipatory military actions, with the possibility that a state that failed to obtain prior Security Council approval would subsequently be able to plead necessity and ask forgiveness. A similar logic was deployed by the Israeli Supreme Court, in a case dealing with "physical means"—which many would describe as torture—in *Public Committee against Torture v. Israel*. Israeli law was interpreted as supplying the security services not with a prior authorization but with a "necessity defense" that could be employed in the context of a criminal prosecution by torture victims. The necessity defense requires a showing that an extraordinary action in violation of the usual rules was justified in the context of a specific set of facts.

Koh concludes by warning that, in the face of "insuperable problems of knowledge, proof, and prediction," any prior authorization of unilateral preventive war is simply too fraught with danger to be contemplated.

Richard Tuck writes on behalf of Hobbesian skepticism with respect to the constraining force of international legality. Not, it should be emphasized, skepticism about the basic principles of morality. For as Tuck argues, drawing on his own important scholarship, Thomas Hobbes joined Hugo Grotius in asserting two fundamental moral principles of universal applicability: one is that people are always entitled to defend themselves against attack, and the other is that they should never inflict unnecessary harm on others. These authors would join Michael Doyle in his view that self-defense can justify preventive war, and not only defensive and preemptive war.

Tuck—not unlike Koh—parts company with Doyle with respect to his expectations about the efficacy of Doyle's four limiting conditions. He notes that the first three conditions propounded by Doyle roughly track the work that is done by the two ideas of reasonable self-defense and no unnecessary harm. Tuck insists, however, that principles such as these, though widely accepted, do little real work for us. Everything turns on how these broad principles are interpreted and applied by actual states in actual circumstances; in such cases, a world of conflict can and does arise with respect to difficult questions concerning how gathering threats should be assessed, and what constitutes a reasonable response.

This leads to Doyle's fourth condition, which turns out to be all-important on Tuck's interpretation. If the principles that underlie lethality, likelihood, and legitimacy (or proportionality) are widely agreeable, with all of the difficulties present in the application in actual circumstances, then the crucial thing is whether it is reasonable to expect different national actors to be capable of agreeing in particular cases, or influencing and moderating one another in the heat of actual impending conflict. On that score, Tuck is skeptical that the UN Security Council or any other actual international forum will prove efficacious. Whereas Doyle holds out the hope that mutual submission to an international forum and serious discussion can both improve decisions and exert some genuine constraints, at least over time, Tuck is highly doubtful that anything short of a state can be efficacious. "Can one imagine," Tuck asks, "the result of such a discussion as having anything like the force of the decrees of a statelike institution or sovereign body?" And in the end, Tuck also pleads that we place our trust in politics rather than any quasi-judicial tribunal.

Jeff McMahan is not principally concerned, as are Koh and Tuck, with the question of whether moral and legal principles will actually constrain political leaders. Rather, he largely agrees with Doyle's argument, but insists that an additional condition is needed to assess whether and when resorts to preventive war are justified morally. He usefully points out, first, that even traditional or orthodox accounts of just war sometimes contain a preventive element. Once a country has made itself liable to military action by itself engaging in an unjust attack, it is liable to defensive force that may be aimed not only at repelling the wrongful attack but also preventing and deterring future wrongful attacks. In this sense, McMahan argues that the traditional view, as expounded by Augustine, Aquinas, and Grotius, allows for the use of force, under proper conditions, "to eliminate more distant threats" from a proven adversary. It is crucial on this view, however, that the justifiability of force aimed at prevention is deployed against a country that has made itself liable to defensive measures by its own actions, and not simply based on the predictions and fears of others.

McMahan takes the argument a step further—as he has in his other writings on war[10]—and argues that questions of moral liability to attack are applicable not only at the collective level, or regarding a state or a country as a whole. We must, McMahan provocatively argues, ask questions about liability to attack in considering just cause for war, *jus ad bellum*, and also in the just conduct of war, *jus in bello*. McMahan argues that individual soldiers are, morally speaking, liable to attack only based on their own actions and commitments, not the actions and commitments of others. Unwilling conscripts and unmobilized conscripts may not be morally liable to being attacked. Political leaders who are responsible for taking a country to war may be morally liable to being killed. McMahan thus suggests that the issue of moral liability to attack must be an in-

---

[10] Jeff McMahan, *The Ethics of Killing in War: The Oxford Uehiro Lectures* (Oxford: Oxford University Press, forthcoming).

dividualized inquiry, as moral liability can flow only from individual actions and commitments for which one is morally responsible. The traditional rules of justice in war have failed to take individualized responsibility seriously, on McMahan's view.

McMahan does not suggest that an individualized inquiry needs to be conducted before any individual is targeted—including each soldier in an opponent's army. This obviously would not be feasible and could easily lead to disaster for a country facing an unjust attack. But he does argue that some generalized judgments can feasibly be made and will be relevant to shaping justifiable military decisions. Thus if we face two armies—one of seasoned volunteers and another of young conscripts—and the defeat of either would help repel an unjust attack, we may have greater reason to target the former. McMahan simply wishes to suggest that a fifth entry should be included in the list of standards propounded by Doyle, namely, individualized liability.

In his concluding response, Doyle argues that while norms such as those he proposes for the international arena cannot be expected to replicate the predictability of domestic politics, they can improve decision making and also post hoc assessment. It is crucial, he insists, for scholars and others to articulate appropriate standards for guiding and assessing the preventive resort to force.

We owe Professor Doyle and his able commentators a great debt for advancing our common conversation about when nations are justified in resorting to armed force.

Striking First

MICHAEL W. DOYLE

When should states go to war in order to protect themselves? When, that is, are they justified in employing either armed force or other warlike coercive measures, such as blockade and sanctions, for anticipatory self-defense?[1] Must they wait, as international law currently holds, for an "armed attack" to have already taken place or to be so imminent that it is, as customary international law holds, "overwhelming" in its necessity and so "imminent" as to leave "no choice of means" and "no moment for deliberation"?[2]

The traditional conception of self-defense allowing only for imminent *preemptive* anticipation of planned attacks is clearly rejected in current U.S. strategic doctrine. Despite attempts to adopt preemptive terminology, President Bush reiterated his and the U.S. government's

---

[1] I am thus interested in the full range of the spectrum of "war"— the enforcement measures in UN Charter Chapter VII, from compulsory sanctions, through blockades and armed actions by land, sea, and air, to invasion and armed occupation.

[2] "Armed attack" is the standard in Article 51 of the Charter of the United Nations. Imminence is the standard defined in U.S. Secretary of State Daniel Webster's famous words in the *Caroline* case in 1842. See John Bassett Moore, *A Digest of International Law*, 217 (GPO, 1906), 2:412; and R. Y. Jennings, *The* Caroline *and McLeod Cases*, 32 Am. J. Int'l L. 82 (1938).

commitment to a much more *preventive* anticipation of threats posed by those who share a "murderous ideology." He declared, on June 28, 2005, at Fort Bragg:

> After September the 11th, I made a commitment to the American people: This nation will not wait to be attacked again. We will defend our freedom. We will take the fight to the enemy.
>
> Iraq is the latest battlefield in this war. Many terrorists who kill innocent men, women, and children on the streets of Baghdad are followers of the same murderous ideology that took the lives of our citizens in New York, in Washington, and Pennsylvania. There is only one course of action against them: to defeat them abroad before they attack us at home.[3]

President Bush is now (winter 2006) focusing on the threat he perceives from Iran. In a recent speech in Salt Lake City to the American Legion convention, he declared: "The world now faces a grave threat from the radical regime in Iran. We know the depth of the suffering that Iran's sponsorship of terrorists has brought. And we can imagine how much worse it would be if Iran were allowed to acquire nuclear weapons." After blam-

---

[3] George W. Bush, "Address to the Nation on the War on Terror from Fort Bragg, North Carolina," *Weekly Compilation of Presidential Documents* 41, no. 26 (28 June 2005): 1079–84; see also George W. Bush, "Remarks to the National Endowment for Democracy," *Weekly Compilation of Presidential Documents* 41, no. 40 (6 October 2005): 1502–8. In his remarks to the National Endowment for Democracy, President Bush claimed, "The murderous ideology of the Islamic radicals is the great challenge of our new century."

ing Iran for supporting Hezbollah violence, supplying the insurgents in Iraq with weapons, and denying basic human rights to its own population, President Bush concluded: "There must be consequences for Iran's defiance [of the UN Security Council resolution mandating a halt to nuclear fuel reprocessing] and we must not allow Iran to develop a nuclear weapon."[4] A few days later, Israeli minister Jacob Edri said that a military strike against Iran, limited to its nuclear facilities, is inevitable before President Bush completes his second term.[5]

In these essays, I will examine the distinction—which the president elides—between acts of *preemption* in the face of an imminent threat of armed attack and acts of *prevention* undertaken in order to forestall, for instance, the acquisition of threatening capabilities. This distinction is a question of *substantive* norms or rules. I will also explore the significance of multilateral authorization by the UN Security Council, which is a question of *procedure* for authorizing the use of force. Thus these essays will explore the ethics, politics, and law of anticipatory self-defense. I will focus both on what the law is and what states should do.

[4] Anne Gearan, Associated Press, "Bush Warns Tehran Anew on Nuclear Weapons Program," August 31, 2006. But at the same time, Russia, China, and Germany all have ruled out the use of force against Iran, while leaving the door open to other sanctions if Iran fails to halt its enrichment of nuclear fuel. Louis Charbonneau, Reuters, "Germany Says Iran Can't Be Allowed to Harm U.N.," September 6, 2006.

[5] "Minister nennt Militärschlag gegen Iran unvermeidbar" [Minister calls military strike against Iran unavoidable], *Die Welt*, September 5, 2006, http://www.welt.de/data/2006/09/05/1024315.html.

In my first essay, I address what I see to be the main problem: both international law, as it is currently formulated, and the Bush Doctrine of prevention are inadequate for today's global security environment. My true aim, however—given those first judgments—is to propose in my second essay better preventive standards for war and warlike measures short of war that would produce more security for the United States and most other states interested in a law-abiding world.

INTERNATIONAL LAW
AND CURRENT STANDARDS

⌘

The problems with existing international law and standards are fourfold: first, the substantive rules are inadequate; second, the Bush Doctrine is subjective and dangerous; third, United Nations procedural rules do not adequately fill the subsequent gap; and fourth, unlike the case of domestic emergencies, breaking the law in the international context—and relying on excuse and mitigation as a framework for order—does not serve well. I will spend most of this essay on the first point.

Substantive Rules:
Self-Defense and Preemptive Self-Defense

Substantive rules for both self-defense and preemptive self-defense exist, but neither set is adequate. Conventionally, states must wait for an "armed attack" to have already occurred, as provided in Article 51 of the UN Charter, or to be so imminent as, under customary international law, to be "overwhelming" in its necessity, leaving "no choice of means" and "no moment for deliberation."[1]

Self-Defense

Even the right of self-defense in the event of an armed attack is not as clear as it might seem. In *Nicaragua v. The United States of America* (the "Nicaragua Case"), the International Court of Justice (ICJ) refused to countenance that the United States was acting in collective self-defense of El Salvador when it used force against Nicaragua. The United States claimed that Nicaragua's provision of weapons and supplies to Salvadoran rebels constituted an "armed attack" to which the United States was merely responding, in support of El Salvador. Noting that the alleged supplying by Nicaragua was itself unproven, the ICJ went on to hold that merely providing weapons to insurgents was not sufficient to qualify as an armed attack, unless (they seemed to imply) its scale was equivalent in effect to a cross-border armed invasion.[2]

In deciding the Nicaragua Case, the ICJ was working, in part, from a "Definition of Aggression" created by

[1] See pp. 12–13, n. 7.

[2] Military and Paramilitary Activities (Nicar. v. U.S.), 1986 I.C.J. 14, 103–5 (June 27). Judge Schwebel, the U.S. judge dissented, arguing that Nicaragua's support for guerrillas in El Salvador was so extensive as to constitute an armed attack, justifying U.S. collective defense of El Salvador, including armed attacks on Nicaragua. Id., 259 (dissenting opinion of Judge Schwebel).

the UN General Assembly. Though its language is not definitive or exclusive, the UN General Assembly declared in 1974 that the "Definition of Aggression"—illicit armed attacks—includes the first use of unauthorized armed force as well as invasion, military occupation, bombardment, blockade of ports or coasts, attacks on land, sea, or air forces, and the sending of armed groups against another state.[3]

Self-defense, however, is more problematic than a laundry list of illicit attacks suggests. A leading text on self-defense defines its legal elements, whether individual or collective, by stipulating that self-defense must be: (1) motivated by defensive concern—that is, it must not be an excuse for looting or a reprisal for past acts; (2) designed to stop an ongoing armed attack, prevent its continuation or reoccurrence, or reverse its consequences (e.g., overthrow an illegal occupation); (3) directed against the responsible party, which was traditionally understood to be a state but since 9/11 may be a terrorist group; (4) limited to the use of only necessary and proportional means; and (5) reported to the Security Council, as required by Article 51.[4]

The first element precludes predation. The second, "ongoing armed attack," element is designed to prohibit unilateral preventive wars. It incorporates preemptive responses to imminent threats, as provided

[3] UN General Assembly Resolution 3314 (XXIX), art. 2, A/RES/ 3314, December 14, 1974.

[4] See the clear and thorough treatment of self-defense in Mary Ellen O'Connell, *International Law and the Use of Force* (New York: Foundation Press, 2005), 240–85.

under customary international law and as intended by the wording of Article 51's "inherent" right of self-defense.[5] The third, "responsible party," element looks for a strong connection between the response and the source of the threat. If the state of origin controlled or supported the attackers, it could be subject to a defensive response. But some have also argued that failure to control the attackers implies culpable responsibility. While the criteria embodied in the fourth element—necessity and proportionality—do constrain legal self-defense, they do not require a "tit-for-tat" response. For example, the United States was not limited to sinking an equivalent number of Japanese battleships in response to Pearl Harbor, but rather could take those measures necessary to end the ongoing threat, even if they included an armed invasion of the aggressor to force it to accept a reliable peace. In these circumstances, proportionality would be secured if the laws of war (*jus in bello*) were followed. Fifth, and finally, the requirement of reporting to the Security Council reflects the council's role as the body primarily responsible for global peace and security. This requirement also reflects the council's authority to order the parties to cease and desist or to intervene if council members determine that such a course would best promote international peace and security.

[5] I follow Oscar Schachter, *The Right of States to Use Armed Force*, 82 Mich. L. Rev. 1620, 1633–35 (1984), and the discussion in Lori Damrosch et al., *International Law: Cases and Materials*, 4th ed. (St. Paul, MN: West Group, 2001), 920–80.

The Caroline *and Preemption*

Customary international law on self-defense undoubtedly includes legitimate preemptive responses. But does it provide a sufficient standard to cover threats that are not imminent? The nineteenth-century case of the *Caroline* provides the widely accepted standard on this issue.[6] Despite its classic status, the incident is a curiously inapt test for preemptive self-defense.

The *Caroline* incident involved a dispute between the United States and the British Empire that occurred in 1837 after an extended crisis in Canadian-American relations. A spate of rebellions had pitted disaffected French-Canadian smallholders against their landlords in Quebec, as well as recent immigrants from the United States against the British landed establishment in the western province of Ontario. Both conflicts leached across the border into the United States, which served as a refuge for the so-called Patriot rebels led by W. L. Mackenzie.

On the night of December 29, 1837, fifty-six Canadian militiamen in seven boats under the command of Royal Navy Commander Andrew Drew set off from Chippewa on the British-Canadian side of the Niagara

---

[6] For a detailed description of the facts in the *Caroline* case, see Kenneth R. Stevens, *Border Diplomacy: The* Caroline *and McLeod Affairs in Anglo-American-Canadian Relations, 1837–1842* (Tuscaloosa: University of Alabama Press, 1989), 1–17; and Jennings, *The* Caroline *and McLeod Cases,* 82–91.

River to destroy an American steamer, the *Caroline*. The Patriot rebels had leased the *Caroline* to supply their forces, and the Canadians believed that the *Caroline* was at Navy Island, a British-Canadian territory in the middle of the river. Colonel Allan MacNab, the commander of the militia in Chippewa, directed Commander Drew to launch his attack of seven boats against the *Caroline* at Navy Island. When Drew found that the *Caroline* was not at Navy Island, however, he and five of his seven boats floated downstream to the U.S. town of Fort Schlosser, where they found the *Caroline* berthed. Drew landed his forces, surprising the sleeping rebels on board the *Caroline,* and seized the ship. He later said that his forces killed five to six rebels, although local reports at the time trumpeted much larger numbers; only one death was later confirmed. Drew and his forces then set the *Caroline* afire and pushed her adrift into the river to plunge over Niagara Falls.

The U.S. diplomats complained to the British about what they perceived to be an unjustified destruction of the *Caroline*. The dispute was eventually resolved through a series of diplomatic notes exchanged between U.S. Secretary of State Daniel Webster and British Minister to Washington Henry Stephen Fox, in 1841. In one of his letters, Secretary of State Webster established four criteria for justifiable preemptive use of force. In Webster's words, justifiable preemptive attack had to be: (1) "overwhelming" in its necessity; (2) leaving "no choice of means"; (3) facing so imminent a threat that there is "no moment for deliberation"; and (4) proportional.[7] While acknowledging the weight and relevance of these factors, Lord Ashburton, the new British envoy, argued in his reply to Webster that the British attack on the *Caroline* did, in fact, meet these criteria. Webster, while not admitting that the incident had been justified, accepted the incongruous British apology.

Colonel MacNab and Commander Drew would have been fully justified in arresting or expelling the rebels on Navy Island—British-Canadian territory after all—and destroying the *Caroline* if they had found it there. But the most comprehensive modern history of the events surrounding the *Caroline* incident correctly concludes that the British-Canadian attack "hardly met the requirements of self-defense set forth in Webster's note of April 24, 1841."[8] We can readily see why. First, the British attack on the *Caroline* was by no means necessary. The British had significantly superior forces; MacNab's forces in Chippewa greatly outnumbered Mackenzie's on Navy Island, with MacNab's forces at 2,500 while estimates of Mackenzie's forces ranged from 150

[7] See Jennings, *The* Caroline *and McLeod Cases*, 89; for a recent analysis of the role international law played in the disputes, see John E. Noyes, "The *Caroline*: International Law Limits on Resort to Force," forthcoming in *International Law Stories*.

[8] Stevens, *Border Diplomacy*, 166. For the wider diplomatic context, see Howard Jones, *To the Webster-Ashburton Treaty: A Study in Anglo-American Relations, 1783–1843* (Chapel Hill: University of North Carolina Press, 1977). We should, however, acknowledge that by nineteenth-century standards, Drew's decision merely to burn the boat—and not the entire town of Fort Schlosser—was a rare act of moderation.

to 800.[9] Second, the U.S. government did not intend to pose a threat to Canada.[10] Instead, President Van Buren had instructed district attorneys to prosecute violators of U.S. neutrality laws and customs officers to restrict incursions. While these efforts were not effective, there was nonetheless goodwill in Washington to improve relations with Great Britain. Third, there was no imminent threat to British-Canadian forces. Government forces earlier in the same month had routed the rebels at Montgomery's Tavern near Toronto. When Drew failed to find the *Caroline* at Navy Island, he could have returned for further orders—as some of his party did. Moreover, the provision of supplies to the Patriots by the *Caroline* did not pose an immediate threat, and there was no other evidence of an impending attack by the Patriots.

Thus even the *Caroline* incident itself did not meet the standards for which the case has become famous. The *Caroline* rules were instead constructed to assert American sovereignty. Despite the gap between the facts and the rules, Webster accepted the British statement (and regrets) in order to restore amity in U.S.-British relations so that more important issues—the northern frontier boundary, for instance—could be addressed. Nevertheless, the criteria delineated in Webster's letter have become the gold standard for justifiable preemption in international law. Indeed, these criteria were applied by the Nuremberg Tribunal to deny Hitler's claim to

[9] Stevens, *Border Diplomacy,* cites both 150 and 800, pp. 10 and 12.

[10] Timothy Kearley, *Raising the Caroline,* 17 Wisc. Int'l L.J. 325 (1999).

justifiable preemption in attacking Norway in 1940[11] and by the Tokyo Tribunal to justify the Netherlands' preemptive declaration of war against Japan in 1941.[12] The *Caroline* standards for imminence were also invoked when the Security Council condemned Israel's preemptive strike against the Iraqi Osirak nuclear reactor in 1981.[13] While there are good reasons for all three of these judgments, it is not clear that either passing or failing the *Caroline* test is one of them.

The *Caroline* standard is too extreme. It is not clear that an attack on U.S. territory was necessary as a matter of imminent self-defense. It is clear that the actual attack was not justified by the principles Webster and Ashburton promulgated. Moreover, the principles themselves are deeply flawed. They justify reflex defensive reactions to imminent threats and nothing more. For instance, they do not leave enough time for states to protect their legitimate interests in self-defense when they still do have some "choice of means," albeit no peaceful ones, and some "time to deliberate" among the dangerous choices left. Extreme *Caroline* conditions are rarely found in reality. With the possible exception of the Netherlands' declaration of war on Japan on December

---

[11] See *Judgment of the International Military Tribunal for the Trial of German Major War Criminals,* Cmd. 6964 (1946), 28–29.

[12] See B.V.A. Röling and C. F. Rüter, eds., *The Tokyo Judgment: The International Military Tribunal for the Far East (I.M.T.F.E.) 29 April 1946–12 November 1948* (Amsterdam: APA-University Press Amsterdam, 1977), 1:382.

[13] See UN Security Council Resolution 487, S/RES/487, June 19, 1981.

8, 1941, accepted by the Tokyo Tribunal, I have not found one example of *Caroline* rules clearly validating an act of preemption. It is not irrelevant that the classic model for justifiable preemption was nothing of the sort. Indeed, the *Caroline* case better illustrates the difficulty of drawing a clear line separating imminent preemption from disallowed prevention.[14]

The deeper problem with the *Caroline* strict standard of imminence is that it is standing in for the more ethically significant considerations of danger and probability. This is the concern that Michael Walzer raises in his influential treatment of the 1967 Six-Day War between Israel and Egypt.[15] Walzer and other scholars have made persuasive arguments that anticipatory uses of force by states are legitimate acts of national self-defense whenever a "failure to do so would seriously risk their territorial integrity or political independence."[16] This more expansive vision of preemption is justified when, Walzer adds, a "sufficient threat" has been demonstrated, in-

---

[14] Indeed, a better defense along these lines was made by the British legal advisers in the Foreign Office: "We feel bound to suggest to your Lordship that the grounds on which we consider the conduct of the British Authorities to be justified is that it was absolutely necessary as a measure of precaution *for the future* and not as a measure of retaliation *for the past*." See Jennings, *The* Caroline *and McLeod Cases*, 87, quoting Report of March 25, 1839, signed by J. Dodson, I. Campbell, R. M. Rolfe, F.O. 83. 2207 (emphasis in original). See also W. Michael Reisman, *International Legal Responses to Terrorism*, 22 Hous. J. Int'l L. 3, 44 (1999).

[15] Michael Walzer, *Just and Unjust Wars: A Moral Argument with Historical Illustrations* (New York: Basic Books, 1977), 80–85.

[16] Ibid., 85.

volving a manifest intent to injure; active preparation to attack on the part of the opponent; and a situation in which waiting significantly magnifies the risk of great harm.[17] These standards are a considerable step forward in matching the virtues of the rule of law with the security of states.

But even these broader standards appear to be under-inclusive for the world in which we now live.[18] Critics of Israeli preemption in the 1967 Six-Day War claimed that Israel knew that Nasser was not planning an attack; that he was merely bluffing.[19] But the heart of Walzer's argument is that Israel could not survive as a small democracy if it had to maintain the mobilization of its military forces in a way that would continue to deter Egypt. If this is the case, "sufficiency" is significantly different from active preparation for a planned attack. But is it any less convincing an argument for action, given that threat environment?

New Insecurities

The dangers posed by contemporary weapons of mass destruction—particularly deliverable nuclear weapons—

[17] Ibid., 81.

[18] Genuine cases of preemptive war have, however, been rare. See Dan Reiter, "Exploding the Powder Keg Myth: Preemptive Wars Almost Never Happen," *International Security* 20, no. 2 (1995): 5. The present circumstances, I will argue, may give rise to a larger number of justifiable occasions.

[19] See the discussion of this issue in Richard K. Betts, "Striking

and the rise of belligerent nonstate actors may well make evidence of "active preparation" excessively difficult to find in time for such threats to be effectively preempted. Moreover, waiting for a sign of an impending attack may pose no obvious increase in danger—that is, until the victimized state is surprised by an attack like that which occurred on 9/11.[20]

Initially, one may argue that in preventing these new threats there is no good reason to dismiss the traditional tools of statecraft. First, *dissuasion,* or nonforcible prevention, can address some long-run threats by altering the strategic environment in which forcible threats thrive. One mode of dissuasion includes "draining the swamp" by strengthening states, upholding the rule of law, and promoting economic opportunities. Some threats can and should be appeased when the claims made are legitimate or capable of being accommodated without significant cost to status quo powers. Permitting Mao's China to take the Chinese seat on the Security Council and Russia to assume the Soviet Union's seat are two such examples. In the past, some terrorist groups or their members (the Stern Gang, the PLO, and the IRA) have been accepted into legitimate politics.[21] Occupation may stimulate terrorist responses and, if so,

---

First: A History of Thankfully Lost Opportunities," *Ethics and International Affairs* 17, no. 1 (2003): 17–24.

[20] See the insightful survey and analysis by James Steinberg, "The Use of Preventive Force as an Element of U.S. National Strategy" (working paper, Princeton Project on National Security, 2006), http://www.wws.princeton.edu/ppns/papers/Steinberg_Preemption.pdf.

[21] For wide-ranging presentations of terrorist and counterterrorist

ending unjust occupations should certainly be addressed in international diplomacy.[22]

Second, other threats can be *denied* though the construction of good defenses. Examples of such defenses today include IAEA inspections to curb nuclear proliferation, enhanced border controls, securing chemical and nuclear stockpiles, and better inspection of containers on ships and baggage on airlines.[23] The UN Security Council adopted a landmark resolution, SCR 1540, on April 28, 2004. The resolution prohibits states from assisting nonstate actors in the acquisition of weapons of mass destruction. But the lack of compliance and international enforcement led to a follow-up resolution two years later, SCR 1673, that reaffirmed the commit-

---

strategies and evolutionary paths, see Audrey Kurth Cronin, "How al-Qaida Ends: The Decline and Demise of Terrorist Groups," *International Security* 31, no. 1 (2006): 7–48; and Andrew H. Kydd and Barbara F. Walter, "The Strategies of Terrorism," *International Security* 31, no. 1 (2006): 49–80.

[22] See Robert Pape, *Dying to Win* (New York: Random House, 2005). Note Pape's argument applies only to suicide terrorism, not all forms of terrorism. Ibid., 9–11. And, even so, critics have countered it in particular cases, noting, for example, the extensive record of terrorism against Israel before the 1967 occupation of the West Bank. See Israel Ministry of Foreign Affairs, "Which Came First—Terrorism or Occupation: Major Arab Terrorist Attacks against Israelis prior to the 1967 Six-Day War," March 31, 2002, http://www.israel-mfa.gov.il/ MFA/Terrorism+Obstacle+to+Peace/Palestinian+terror+before+2000/ Which+Came+First-+Terrorism+or+Occupation+-+Major.htm.

[23] In September 2006, the General Assembly endorsed an enhanced and internationally funded strategy to improve border controls. See Nick Wadhams, Associated Press, "U.N. General Assembly Adopts New Counterterrorism Strategy," September 8, 2006. To

ment—but also without providing international enforcement. Some have even suggested that missile defenses, which were and are unlikely to work against a massive Soviet-style attack, could successfully deny a much more limited attack, say by North Korea or Iran.[24]

Third, where denial is difficult, *deterrence* may work. Deterrence held the Soviet threat—a much more significant threat than any today—at bay throughout the Cold War, and deterrence will effectively prevent the realization of many of the threats we face today (as I discuss below).[25] Other forms of coercive diplomacy including economic embargoes can restrain the development of threatening capacity or signal the costs that will be imposed if threats continue.[26]

Nonetheless, today's more salient threats do not appear to be fully amenable to such traditional counterstrategies. Preventive responses that involve unilateral armed attack or multilateral enforcement measures may be necessary. These contravene peaceful foreign relations and range from multilateral economic sanctions

date, Russia has eliminated just 3 percent of its toxic chemical stockpile, as opposed to 39 percent destroyed by the United States, which is home to the second-largest stockpile. Judith Ingram, Associated Press, "Russia Opens Weapons Destruction Plant," September 8, 2006.

[24] I owe this suggestion to Ruth Wedgwood.

[25] For an eloquent defense of deterrence and an argument that its utility has been radically underestimated by the Bush administration, see Ian Shapiro, *Containment: Rebuilding a Strategy against Global Terror* (Princeton: Princeton University Press, 2007).

[26] Alexander George, *Forceful Persuasion* (Washington, DC: U.S. Institute of Peace, 1991).

through blockades to intervention and all-out armed invasion.

Some forms of *terrorism,* for example, are hard to prevent through long-term dissuasive means such as economic development—the motivations for terrorists are rarely lack of other job opportunities.[27] It is also particularly difficult to defend open societies against terrorism through denial—by eliminating vulnerabilities—partly because of the cost of comprehensive protection and partly because such societies usually reject the pervasive police measures that the most effective forms of counterterrorism employ (there were, for example, few terrorist incidents in Stalin's Soviet Union or Mao's China, other than those committed by the state).[28] Instead, active preventive measures seem to be the better strategy today. Senator Sam Nunn, a widely respected expert on securing loose nukes and nuclear material, has said: "Acquiring weapons and materials is the hardest step

[27] See Alberto Abadie, "Poverty, Political Freedom, and the Roots of Terrorism" (National Bureau of Economic Research Working Paper No. 10859, 2004), http://www.nber.org/papers/w10859; Alan B. Krueger and Jitka Maleckova, "Education, Poverty and Terrorism: Is There a Causal Connection?" *Journal of Economic Perspective* 17, no. 4 (2003): 119–44.

[28] On the vulnerability of the United States to ordinary shipments of nuclear and other chemical and biological dangerous materials, see Graham Allison, *Nuclear Terrorism: The Ultimate Preventable Catastrophe* (New York: Times Books, 2004), 104–20. Nonetheless, a terrorist nuclear bomb or biological attack is the least likely threat; much more feasible for a terrorist attack would be a dirty bomb (radioactive material dispersed by a conventional explosion) with wide and harmful effects.

for terrorists to take, and the easiest for us to stop. By contrast every subsequent step in the process is easier for the terrorists to take, and harder for us to stop."[29] This reasoning has led Graham Allison, another widely respected expert, to recommend a preventive—and co-operative, multilateral—strategy to ensure "No Loose Nukes," "No New Nascent Nukes," and "No New Nuclear Weapons States."[30]

Deterrence may similarly fail to forestall some of today's threats. It is generally understood that terrorists are difficult to deter. Today's most virulent terrorist campaigns (al Qaeda, Hamas, Hezbollah, Tamil Tigers, and others) recruit suicide bombers for so-called martyrdom operations. Deterrent retaliation is for them, in effect, a reward, not a punishment. These threats are also difficult to deter because they lack a state with the stakes vulnerable to deterrent retaliation that could facilitate responsible decision making. Failed states offer space for the operation of terrorist groups, but terrorist groups have no incentive to maintain law and order, and the nominal authorities are incapable of doing so. Western Pakistan is such a refuge today. There are also reasonable worries that Iraq is deteriorating into such a situation. A particularly disturbing scenario would be the consequences of a failed nuclear state. What should happen if the government of Kim Jong-il or Pervez Musharaff suddenly collapsed, leaving control of their nuclear

---

[29] Senator Sam Nunn, "Preventing Catastrophic Terrorism" (lecture, International Institute for Strategic Studies, London, January 20, 2003), quoted in Allison, *Nuclear Terrorism*, 199.

[30] Allison, *Nuclear Terrorism*, 140–75.

arsenals up for grabs?[31] Lastly, terrorist groups tend to operate clandestinely through what the Bush administration has called "shadowy networks of individuals" that, unlike armies massing near a frontier, do not leave a large enough footprint to be susceptible to imminent detection or targeting.

Finally, while so called *rogue states* may be deterrable, many are only partially deterrable, or deterrable at too high a moral cost. Few believe that Saddam Hussein was, or today that Kim Jong-il is, likely to attack the United States. Saddam displayed rational behavior during the first Persian Gulf War in 1990 when he decided not to use chemical or biological weapons against either the U.S.-led coalition or Israel, despite the defeat he should have known was likely to ensue. Saddam correctly inferred that such an act would lead to a massive response likely to be fatal—not just to his regime, but to himself.[32]

But a Saddam Hussein with nuclear weapons would have been an extremely dangerous actor in the Middle East, with costly implications that would have extended far beyond the region. Saddam could have distributed nuclear weapons or nuclear material to terrorists with the aim of disrupting the West, counting on the plethora of loose nukes to shield him from identification as the

[31] See a thoughtful discussion of these scenarios in Michael O'Hanlon, "Dealing with the Collapse of a Nuclear-Armed State: The Case of North Korea and Pakistan" (working paper, Princeton Project on National Security, Princeton, 2006), http://www.wws.princeton.edu/ppns/papers/ohanlon.pdf.

[32] John J. Mearsheimer and Stephen M. Walt, op-ed, "Keeping Saddam Hussein in a Box," *New York Times,* February 2, 2003, A15.

supplier. More rationally and directly, he might have threatened to employ them in the region to destroy the Saudi oil fields unless the international community tolerated his occupation of Kuwait. The destruction of the oil fields would have sent the world economy into a 1930s-scale depression. And, on the other hand, leaving Saddam Hussein in possession of Kuwait would have intimidated the entire region, thereby allowing him to create oil shocks at will. The United States could readily have threatened to destroy Baghdad with a nuclear detonation. But would such a threat have been credible given that hundreds of thousands of innocent Iraqi civilians would have been killed, and that Saddam Hussein would have succeeded in destroying the oil fields in any case?[33] It was therefore important to prevent Saddam Hussein from acquiring deliverable nuclear weapons. I will come to the question of *how* a bit later.

In short, the success of deterring the Soviet Union in the Cold War is misleading. The Soviets, unlike al Qaeda but like Saddam Hussein and Kim Jong-il, were rationally deterrable. But unlike Saddam Hussein and Kim Jong-il (and perhaps the Iranians) they were also satisfied. The Soviets were both rational and satisfied (though some of their actions seemed to disprove this, as discussed below). By 1945 they had acquired as much of Eastern Europe as they could digest. Saddam Hussein

[33] See the discussion in Kenneth M. Pollack, *The Threatening Storm: The Case for Invading Iraq* (New York: Random House, 2002), 243–80. This well-informed and influential book helped disarm much of the resistance to the invasion pressure mounted by the Bush administration.

was not and Kim Jong-il and Mahmood Ahmedinejad do not appear to be satisfied. In their hands, WMD can become an umbrella for subversion and aggression.

The Bush Doctrine of "Preemption," Actually Prevention

The contemporary alternative to traditional international law is the Bush Doctrine. In its *National Security Strategy,* issued in September 2002, the Bush administration announced a doctrine of "preemptive" actions designed (in fact) to *prevent* "our enemies from threatening us, our allies, and our friends, with weapons of mass destruction." The document elaborated that "[t]he greater the threat, the greater is the risk of inaction—and the more compelling the case for taking anticipatory action to defend ourselves, even if uncertainty exists as to the time and place of the enemy attack."[34] This became, in Vice President Dick Cheney's words, the "one percent doctrine," which connoted that even a 1 percent chance of an attack with weapons of mass destruction constituted an unacceptable risk.[35] The potential harm and increased likelihood of such an attack today make the risk to the United States unbearable.

[34] National Security Council, *The National Security Strategy of the United States of America* (Washington, DC, 2002), 1, http://www.whitehouse.gov/nsc/nss.pdf.

[35] See Ron Suskind, *The One Percent Doctrine: Deep Inside America's Pursuit of Its Enemies since 9/11* (New York: Simon & Schuster, 2006), 62.

One immediate problem with the Bush administration's line of reasoning is that the world is full of risks from those with "murderous ideologies," but resources are limited. Dangers must be balanced against the costs of responding to them and prioritized to determine which should be handled first, and which can wait.

There is another problem with allowing one state to adopt a standard that is as subjective and open-ended as the Bush administration's identification of threats. Invoking the principle of sovereign equality, other states will claim an equivalent right to act on their equivalently arbitrary threat suspicions, which ultimately would be an invitation to chaos.[36] Unless all states agree on what constitutes a specific threat—and they almost never do—every state will be preempting every other state's preventive strikes.[37]

---

[36] Vattel defined both the principle and the consequences: "A dwarf is as much a man as a giant; a small republic is no less a sovereign state than the most powerful kingdom. By a necessary consequence of that equality, whatever is lawful for one nation, is equally lawful for any other; and whatever is unjustifiable in the one, is equally so in the other." Emmerich de Vattel, "Preliminaries," in *The Law of Nations*, 18–19 (Philadelphia: T. & J. W. Johnson, 1867), lxiii. For an insightful discussion of sovereign equality, see Thomas H. Lee, "International Law, International Relations Theory, and Preemptive War: The Vitality of Sovereign Equality Today," *Law and Contemporary Problems* 67, no. 4 (2004): 147–67; and David J. Luban, "Preventive War," *Philosophy and Public Affairs* 32, no. 3 (2004): 207–48.

[37] This is called the "security dilemma" and the "chicken game" in international politics. The former explains arms races as owing to the inability to distinguish defensive arming from offensive arming.

Recognizing this dilemma, the Bush Doctrine attempts to depict the targets of its preventive strategy as followers of "murderous ideologies" and members of an "axis of evil,"[38] and particularly threats that are "grave and growing."[39] But the underlying threats referred to by the president lack the specificity to justify these categories.[40] Preventive arguments similar to the ones made by President Bush could have been made—and related ones were—to justify a preventive attack on the Soviet Union and China during the Cold War when they were about to acquire atomic weapons.[41] But in retrospect, most regard it as fortunate that the Cold War played itself out as a "cold" deterrent struggle rather than a "hot" prevention.

The latter explains the brinksmanship that can result in escalation to war as prompted by the need to demonstrate resolve in order to avoid exploitation. See Robert Jervis, "Cooperation under the Security Dilemma," *World Politics* 30, no. 2 (1978): 167–214. The basic theme is that the security dilemma varies and is not constant.

[38] See George W. Bush, "Address before a Joint Session of the Congress on the State of the Union," *Weekly Compilation of Presidential Documents* 38, no. 5 (January 29, 2002): 133–39.

[39] See, e.g., George W. Bush, radio address, "Iraqi Regime Danger to America Is 'Grave and Growing,'" *Weekly Compilation of Presidential Documents* 38, no. 40 (October 5, 2002): 1656–57. Also available at http://www.whitehouse.gov/news/releases/2002/10/20021005.html.

[40] Indeed one of President Bush's former speechwriters has suggested that North Korea was added to Iraq and Iran to make the "Axis" into three—World War II–style (Germany, Italy, and Japan). See David Frum, *The Right Man: The Surprise Presidency of George W. Bush* (New York: Random House, 2003), 231–39.

[41] See Betts, "Striking First," 21–22.

If the Bush Doctrine were adopted globally today, it could open the door to wars between Pakistan and India and perhaps even China and Taiwan.[42] Presently, while the administration considers North Korea's and Iran's nuclear programs to be threats, the North Korean and the Iranian regimes undoubtedly consider the Bush regime to be a threat. Is each to be accorded the right to attack preventively? Even while Hezbollah leader Sheikh Hassan Nasrallah recently claimed his organization would not have begun the July 2006 war against Israel if it had known how much devastation would be incurred by Lebanon, he went on to claim that Hezbollah's attacks had preemptively spared Lebanon the worse onslaught that Israel was planning for September or October.[43]

Given all the uncertainties involved in measuring long-run intentions and capabilities, preventive doctrines that lack impartial standards seem to court not only extreme international instability, but a radical weakening of moral restraints. In the end, too many people would wind up being killed on what might be no better than self-serving and poorly informed hunches of political leaders.

Even traditional standards of self-defense are subject to abuse. Indeed, in February 1848, then-Representative

[42] For a good critique of the Bush Doctrine along these lines, see Neta Crawford, "The Slippery Slope to Preventive War," *Ethics and International Affairs* 17, no. 1 (2003): 30–36.

[43] Borzou Daragahi, "Hezbollah Leader Regrets Kidnapping Israeli Soldiers," *Cincinnati Post*, August 28, 2006, A14 (recounting remarks make by Nasrallah during a two-hour interview on the New TV network).

Abraham Lincoln famously condemned President Polk's unsubstantiated claim that Mexico had attacked the United States, justifying the war for Texas. "Allow the President," Lincoln said, "to invade a neighboring nation, whenever he shall deem it necessary to repel an invasion and you allow him to do so whenever he may choose to say he deems it necessary for such purpose— and you allow him to make war at pleasure. . . . If, today, he should choose to say he thinks it necessary to invade Canada to prevent the British from invading us, how could you stop him? You may say to him, 'I see no probability of the British invading us'; but he will say to you, 'Be silent; I see it, if you don't.' " Subjective and abstract standards of prevention are subject to unverifiable claims that are very difficult to contest. They are much too likely to be self-serving, promoting narrow partisan advantages.[44]

One response to these problems is to cite American exceptionalism; that is to say that the United States is special—a hegemonic state with hegemonic responsibilities and hegemonic capabilities. The rights it claims to protect others by protecting itself cannot be generalized to weaker states. But few states acknowledge this special license for the United States. Moreover, it is not even clear that the American people would accept the burdens of actually policing the world that would accompany this status if the claim to it were made in good faith.[45]

[44] Quoted in Arthur Schlesinger, Jr., "Bush's Thousand Days," *Washington Post,* April 24, 2006, A17.

[45] David Luban considers this in his "Preventive War" and rejects it for a number of reasons, including the ones noted above.

MICHAEL W. DOYLE

Procedural Remedies at the Security Council

We usually address the problems of ex ante uncertainty, incomplete information, and motivated bias in interpretation through *procedural* standards. We subject these judgments to structured deliberation and contestation in the presence of impartial (or at least multiple) decision-makers—in the classic phrase, in order to reflect a decent respect for the opinions of mankind.

On the one hand, under current international law, unilateral prevention is illegal. On the other, multilateral prevention is not only legal; it must be considered whenever threats arise. The process of multilateral decision making embedded in the UN Security Council by Article 39 of Chapter VII gives the council the authority to—indeed, requires that the council "shall"—"determine the existence of *any* threat to the peace, breach of the peace or act of aggression" and take whatever action, including coercive embargoes and forcible measures by land, air, or sea, that the council sees fit.[46] The council is specifically empowered not merely to respond to breaches of the peace and acts of aggression that have occurred, but to address "threats" before they materialize—and not just imminent threats, but "any" threats. Such coercive measures are automatically binding on all UN member states.[47] So any time a state can get a vote of nine out of fifteen members, including no vetoes from the Permanent Five—the United States, Russia, France,

[46] UN Charter art. 39 (emphasis added).
[47] Ibid., art. 25.

30

the United Kingdom, and China—then legitimate and fully legal preventive action may be undertaken. Many of the strongest critics and proponents of forceful prevention—like Monsieur Jourdain, Molière's *bourgeois gentilhomme,* who discovered he had been speaking prose—seem unaware of its legality. The real issues are these: who can authorize it, and what standards should govern it.

This procedural solution has recently been reaffirmed as an adequate response to the current challenges of counterterrorism and weapons of mass destruction proliferation in the report of the secretary-general's eminent High-level Panel on Threats, Challenges and Change.[48] The Security Council process solution can be justified both as obligatory international law and as a legitimate quasi-deliberative, quasi-representative process.

Procedural legitimacy is enhanced by additional multilateral deliberation and by the fact that a national government seeking authorization for preventive measures must persuade at least nine members of the Security Council to vote for its cause. The diversity of the other council member states requires that the arguments for

---

[48] UN Secretary-General, *Report of the Secretary-General's High-level Panel on Threats, Challenges and Change* (2004), 63–67, http://www.un.org/secureworld/report2.pdf. The panel included eminent statespersons such as former U.S. National Security Adviser Brent Scowcroft, former UN High Commissioner for Refugees Sadako Ogata, and others. The panel reaffirmed traditional just war standards of proportionality and last resort as substantive guidelines. As a UN-appointed panel, it not surprisingly also limited preventive self-defense to prior Security Council authorization. See ibid., ¶191.

preventive action must appeal beyond the narrow confines of interest, ideology, and culture of a single state. At a minimum, the Permanent Five must be persuaded. They include one hyperpower and four lesser powers; Asian (China) and Western states; Confucian, Orthodox, and Christian religious traditions; statist (China and Russia) and more laissez-faire (United States) and social democratic (France and the United Kingdom) economies. In addition to the Permanent Five, the Security Council includes ten elected and often much less powerful and wealthy states, which by tradition include states from Latin America, Africa, and the remainder of Asia and Europe. Any seven of those ten can block a Security Council authorization.[49]

I do not wish to portray this process as anything close to an "ideal speech situation."[50] The Security Council is an arena for real politics when important issues arise. Pressure is exercised by the powerful states on those less powerful (in many ways, including in famous cases large sums of foreign aid), and some states, most obviously the United States, have "outside options" to act unilaterally (though without legal authorization) that give additional weight to their requests.[51] Yet the oppo-

[49] See Thomas Franck, *Fairness in International Law and Institutions* (Oxford: Clarendon Press, 1995) (discussing the "global jury").

[50] As, for example, outlined in Jürgen Habermas, *The Theory of Communicative Action,* trans. Thomas McCarthy (Boston: Beacon Press, 1984), where fair procedure becomes a formal guarantee of fair outcome.

[51] On the hegemonic possibilities of U.S. influence in the UN Security Council, see José E. Alvarez, *International Organizations as*

site error is to see the council as a mere rubber stamp for U.S. interests. The failure of the United States to secure a second council vote against Iraq—one that would have authorized an armed intervention—despite a large investment of positive and negative inducements by the Bush administration, is evidence that the process is no rubber stamp for the United States.

The Security Council process seems a neat and satisfactory solution but for two problems: first, the council has in numerous instances in the past behaved irresponsibly—failed to authorize the use of force when it was arguably justified; and second, the council lacks substantively adequate standards to guide its deliberations concerning when it should authorize preventive force.

With respect to the first problem, I have in mind the failure to act in a timely way to address two humanitarian emergencies, Kosovo and Rwanda, and various lesser decisions.[52] As scholars Tom Farer and Robert

---

Law-makers (New York: Oxford University Press, 2005), 199–216; and Erik Voeten, "The Strategic Use of Liberal Internationalism: Libya and the U.N. Sanctions, 1992–2003," *International Organization* 59, no. 3 (2005): 500–503.

[52] Lesser decisions include failures to renew the mandated Macedonian peace operation because Macedonia had established relations with Taiwan, leading to Chinese retaliation with a veto. But let me hasten to add that China has cast by far the fewest vetoes between 1946 and 1997 (a total of 4). The USSR/Russia and the United States lead the league with 116 and 72, respectively. The total is 202 in that period. See Sydney D. Bailey and Sam Daws, *The Procedure of the U.N. Security Council*, 3rd ed. (Oxford: Clarendon Press, 1998), 231–39. As important, permanent members have threatened to use the veto, and the threat is often enough to derail action on an issue.

Keohane and Allen Buchanan have argued, the Security Council sometimes fails to take into account the legitimate security needs of states when the council is stymied by, for example, an irresponsible veto.[53] When should states feel that preventive action is legitimate *without* Security Council authorization? Procedural standards are not a sufficient answer.

With respect to the second problem, rule of law and global public comity require substantive deliberation in the Security Council. The council itself requires standards for decisions that go beyond "anything" that can assemble the relevant nine votes out of fifteen. Not every justification can be deemed legitimate prevention. Simi-

---

[53] Farer makes a persuasive case for derogation to regional organization and even individual state action. He adds that in order to avoid exploitative recourses to unjustified force, such derogations should be subject to retroactive judicial assessment by the International Court of Justice. See Tom Farer, "A Paradigm of Legitimate Intervention," in *Enforcing Restraint: Collective Intervention in Internal Conflicts*, ed. Lori Fisler Damrosch (New York: Council on Foreign Relations Press, 1993), 316. Keohane and Buchanan, in addition to deepening Farer's analysis, make a case for devolving such decisions to coalitions of democratic states whose constitutional procedures and democratic principles arguably make them better guarantors of humanitarian principles. Equivalent arguments can be made for anticipatory self-defense. See Allen Buchanan and Robert O. Keohane, "The Preventive Use of Force: A Cosmopolitan Institutional Proposal," *Ethics and International Affairs* 18, no. 1 (2004): 1–22. Cornelius Bjola makes similar arguments, focusing on communicative deliberation. See Cornelius Bjola, "Legitimating the Use of Force in International Politics: A Communicative Action Perspective," *European Journal of International Relations* 11, no. 2 (2005): 266–303.

larly, states that decide to bypass the Security Council or take preventive measures without council authorization will need to justify those decisions to both international and domestic publics, and, if Farer's and Buchanan and Keohane's procedural standards are adopted, to a subsequent international tribunal.

The Security Council has a long, and in many cases praiseworthy, record of acting preventively on the basis of Chapter VII against perceived "threats to the peace" that did not constitute imminent attacks. For instance, the council imposed obligatory sanctions on Rhodesia (1966) and South Africa (1977), which were the equivalents of arms blockades.[54] Drawing up a list just three years into the expansion of council activity that characterized the post–Cold War period, Lori Damrosch has identified a wide range of other triggers for successful Chapter VII determinations of threats against the peace, including genocide, ethnic cleansing, and war crimes (Former Republic of Yugoslavia, Iraq, Liberia); interference with the delivery of humanitarian supplies (Former Republic of Yugoslavia, Iraq, Somalia); violations of cease-fires (Former Republic of Yugoslavia, Liberia, Cambodia); collapse of civil order (Liberia, Somalia); and coups against democratic governments (Haiti).[55]

Are there standards we can derive from this record that suggest how the Security Council should decide whether the next putative emergency justifies preven-

[54] UN Security Council Resolution 418, S/RES/418, November 4, 1977.

[55] Lori Fisler Damrosch, introduction to *Enforcing Restraint*, 10–14.

tion? Considerable progress has been made in identifying the specifically humanitarian standards that should trigger a "Responsibility to Protect" by the Security Council, and in describing considerations that should be taken into account in authorizing forcible measures.[56] Security Council practice, however, has merged the two. Is it possible to separate out distinct principles for individual or collective self-defense from the wider set of justifications that shape humanitarian action?[57] Rather than reinvent, our real task is to refine the proper standards and show how they apply in contentious cases, judging which cases should serve as positive and negative models for preventive action. I address this challenge in the following essay.

Excuse and Mitigation

Finally, Thomas Franck and other leading scholars have suggested that we should not change the law for preemptive or preventive self-defense because the need is so rare and prevention is so vulnerable to abuse. Instead, under the arguably extreme circumstances where preventive self-defense would be justified, we are better off acknowledging that states will break the taboo against

[56] See UN General Assembly Resolution 60/1, "2005 World Summit Outcome," ¶¶38–41, A/RES/60/1, October 24, 2005.

[57] Separating the two is more difficult. The Security Council will want to reference collective self-defense in humanitarian emergencies because Chapter VII authorization is limited to threats or acts that breach international peace and security, not human rights.

preventive use of force out of "necessity," that we will want to condemn them for the violation; but that the moral circumstances are such that their act will be excused and their punishment mitigated.[58] Parents who steal food to feed their starving children are rarely punished. And yet we do not enact a separate criminal law for starving families.[59]

This policy would be a completely acceptable recourse if decisions to prevent or not prevent were readily reversible and the victim of wrongful prevention or wrongful abstention could be adequately compensated. Grocery

[58] See Thomas M. Franck, *The Use of Force in International Law,* 11 Tul. J. Int'l & Comp. L. 7, 13 (2003) (allowing for the "flexible application of existing rules, in accordance with ... contextual exigencies and with narrow exceptions for situations of extreme necessity"), and Richard Gardner, *Neither Bush nor the Jurisprudes,* 97 Am. J Int'l. L. 585 (2003). See also William C. Bradford, *"The Duty to Defend Them": A Natural Law Justification for the Bush Doctrine of Preventive War,* 79 Notre Dame L.R. 1365, 1395 & n.102 (2004). Bradford notes that some advocates of this approach have characterized the necessity standard as a defense against what would otherwise be unlawful conduct. This approach offers the benefit of preserving what they claim is a general prohibition against anticipatory self-defense that could be abrogated only in cases of genuine peril such as terrorists obtaining WMD. See also John-Alex Romano, *Combating Terrorism and Weapons of Mass Destruction: Reviving the Doctrine of a State of Necessity,* 87 Geo. L.J. 1023, 1025–26 (1999) (proposing a necessity-based standard that would "preclud[e] the wrongfulness" of anticipatory self-defense).

[59] U.S. criminal law anticipates that some otherwise illegal acts are justified if the actor believes them to be necessary to avoid an equal or greater harm to himself or another. See, e.g., Model Penal Code 3.02 cmt. 1 (1985).

stores can be compensated for the food starving families steal. Countries that have been invaded, occupied, and perhaps devastated by wrongful prevention or wrongful abstention can rarely be adequately compensated.

Also, the policy might be justified if the need to consider whether prevention is justified were really that rare a phenomenon. Unfortunately, preventive acts in the international system are far from the extreme. The Security Council record mentioned above is one indication of multiple legal acts of multilateral prevention authorized under Article 39. But we can also find a long record of unilateral preventive war.

Marc Trachtenberg has provided accounts of numerous instances in the postwar period when prevention has been advocated, when it has shaped policy, and when it has been undertaken. Indeed, preventive rollback formed the core of the national security doctrine adopted by the United States in *NSC-68*.[60] Several eminent statesmen at one time or another prescribed it. Winston Churchill, Charles de Gaulle, Paul Nitze (the strategist who authored *NSC-68*), and President Truman all mused about the use of preventive force, as did President Eisenhower, who asked whether "our duty to future generations did not require us to *initiate* war at the most propitious moment that we could designate."[61] Fortunately Eisenhower chose otherwise—although had there been a Soviet attack, we might now think differently.

[60] National Security Council, *NSC-68: United States Objectives and Programs for National Security* (Washington, DC, 1950), http://www.mtholyoke.edu/acad/intrel/nsc-68/nsc68-1.htm.

[61] See the fascinating paper by Marc Trachtenberg, "Preventive

The idea of preventive war was also abused and exploited as many, if not more, times: by Hitler against Poland, by Tojo against the United States at Pearl Harbor, and in numerous covert operations by the United States and the USSR throughout the Cold War (e.g., Guatemala, Bay of Pigs, Hungary, Czechoslovakia, etc.). Lest this seem a peculiarity of the Cold War, it is worth noting that prevention was the rule rather than the exception in the asymmetric warfare between colonial powers and the societies in Africa and Asia with which they came in contact. The frequency of these wars garnered a special literature focusing on the "Turbulent Frontier."[62] John Gaddis has recounted the long record of prevention that characterized U.S. security policy in the nineteenth century and has argued that the strategic circumstances of

---

War and U.S. Foreign Policy" (unpublished manuscript on file with author, December 28, 2005), 7, quoting "Memorandum by the President to the Secretary of State" (Washington, DC, September 8, 1953), as reprinted in U.S. Department of State, *Foreign Relations of the United States 1952–1954*, vol. 2, pt. 1 (Washington, DC: GPO, 1954), 461 (emphasis in original). Trachtenberg's paper, together with the papers by Crawford and Luban cited from other sources here, and other valuable papers too late to be included in this discussion have just appeared in Henry Shue and David Rodin, eds., *Preemption: Military Action and Moral Justification* (Oxford University Press, 2007).

[62] I survey this issue in Michael W. Doyle, *Empires* (Ithaca, NY: Cornell University Press, 1986), 34–48. See also John S. Galbraith, "The 'Turbulent Frontier' as a Factor in British Expansion," *Comparative Studies in Society and History* 2, no. 2 (1960): 150–68; and for French West Africa, see Christopher M. Andrew and A. S. Kanya-Forstner, *The Climax of French Imperial Expansion, 1914–1924* (Stanford, CA: Stanford University Press, 1981).

the post–Cold War world have analogous features that raise a new logic favoring prevention.[63]

Put these together and we retain good reasons to keep the law as simple, as bright a line as possible, in order to discourage self-serving interpretation.[64] As Tom Franck and others have argued, the *Caroline* rule for unilateral preemption and Security Council authorization for multilateral prevention should stand. But at the same time, rather than excuses, we will want guidelines—preventive standards—that will inform debates at the Security Council and guide officials when they face unusual circumstances that seem to warrant an exception. Officials will benefit from standards that, should they prove justified in fact, will or would excuse and mitigate punishment. Having these standards, moreover, should limit the range of likely exceptions and (as will be noted in the following essay) initiate a dialogue, both national and international, that allocates responsibility and accountability between officials and publics when those extreme circumstances arise. One must also acknowledge that to the extent that these defenses are successful—winning the support of publics both national and international, and informing the choices of other states as matters of what rightful conduct requires—they will begin to shape the content of customary international law, just as the *Caroline* doctrine did for the times in which it was appropriate.

[63] See John Lewis Gaddis, *Surprise, Security, and the American Experience* (Cambridge, MA: Harvard University Press, 2004).

[64] My views on this have been influenced by helpful comments made by Harold Koh on the lectures delivered on November 8–9, 2006.

Conclusion

To summarize, the case for new standards for prevention boils down to this: The UN Charter authorizes the Security Council to prevent, but we should not write the Security Council a blank check. It needs a jurisprudence of prevention. Moreover, the council will sometimes fail to behave responsibly. We then have to decide when a state can justifiably engage in unilateral preventive self-defense before international law would currently allow—that is, before an attack is so obvious and imminent as to be overwhelming and leaving no moment for deliberation.

If this is the case, then we need new standards to decide how to act. The danger in medical terms is too many likely false positives and false negatives.[65] In academia we are accustomed to leaning toward the danger of false positives. We want to create a high bar to tenured employment. But in medicine, the dangers are more symmetrical:

> False positives in that the patient is diagnosed with lung cancer and prescribed chemotherapy, when instead he actually has a chest cold;

> False negatives when he is diagnosed with a chest cold and prescribed cough drops when he has lung cancer.

Today, as in medicine, states emulating the Bush Doctrine may wind up invading states preventively when

[65] See Alan M. Dershowitz, *Preemption: A Knife That Cuts Both Ways* (New York: W. W. Norton, 2006), 17.

they pose no likely threat of aggressive attack and could have been deterred and contained. Alternatively, states and armed groups will be tolerated or protected by multilateral stalemate in the Security Council when in fact they should have been arrested, conquered, or coercively sanctioned, sparing innocent victims a 9/11 or a global war on the scale of World War II. I next turn to what I will argue are better standards for prevention.

STANDARDS

I suggested in my first essay that traditional preemption is too strict and the Bush administration's expansive prevention is too loose. In what follows, I propose to recommend four standards for anticipatory self-defense that will address the problems of underinclusiveness and overinclusiveness that I have identified.

It makes sense to limit legal prevention procedurally to actions authorized by the Security Council and legal preemption to actions substantively in accord with the *Caroline* doctrine. But we need to go beyond both. We need substantive preventive standards in order to inform Security Council debates. We also need both substantive and procedural standards in order to decide upon the rare circumstances in which we will want to authorize unilateral prevention.

To do this we need to supplement defenses of preventive war made as a matter of general, philosophic principle. I will propose four standards and illustrate the operation of these standards in contentious cases. These standards will call for further specificity beyond what my essays can possibly provide, but I think they put us on the right track. Ultimately, I want to construct a jurisprudence, derived from cases, that the Security Council should draw upon when it deliberates the question of when to authorize preventive measures under Article 39. This same jurisprudence will serve, in exceptional circumstances, to determine when states should be permitted to undertake forcible prevention if the Security Council fails to authorize their use of force.

General Principles

Compared to the deeply divided views characterizing the legal community and many political scientists, a remarkably large and significant group of moral philosophers finds the theory of preventive war relatively unproblematic. The philosophers condemn many alleged preventive wars—including, for example, the war in Iraq—but the theory troubles them less than the law troubles the lawyers, or the strategy troubles many political scientists.

The basic insight is captured in the famous remark that Secretary of State Elihu Root made in 1914 on the eve of World War I. Secretary Root said that the right of self-protection must allow a state "to protect itself by preventing a condition of affairs in which it will be too late to protect itself."[1] The answer is so obvious that

[1] Elihu Root, *The Real Monroe Doctrine,* 8 Am. J. Int'l L. 427, 432 (1914), cited in Ruth Wedgwood, *The Fall of Saddam Hussein: Security Council Mandates and Preemptive Self-Defense,* 97 Am. J. Int'l L. 576 (2003).

many philosophers, including Whitley Kaufman, reverse the question: "If an enemy is planning an unjust attack against your citizens, and it is within your power to prevent it, why should you *not* act preventively?"[2]

The insights of the moral philosophers are reflected in Judge Learned Hand's famous interpretation of the "clear and present danger" rule, when he articulated a probabilistic standard to justify some restrictions on free speech.[3] Alan Dershowitz has generalized the Hand rule in a formulation for preventive war. Dershowitz asks whether "the seriousness of the contemplated harm, discounted by the unlikelihood that it would occur in the absence of preemption [really, prevention], would be greater than the likelihood of the harms caused by successful preemption [prevention], discounted by the likelihood (and costs) of failed (and successful) preemption [prevention]."[4]

Unfortunately, however, in addition to being more than a mouthful, this rule provides little guidance. It does not tell us nearly enough about how to begin to identify

[2] Whitley Kaufman, "What's Wrong with Preventive War? The Moral and Legal Basis for the Preventive Use of Force," *Ethics and International Affairs* 19, no. 3 (2005): 29 (emphasis in original). See also Luban, "Preventive War"; and Jeff McMahan, "Just Cause for War," *Ethics and International Affairs,* 19, no. 3 (2005): 14–15. Thus who or what has the right to authorize prevention is a key question, as discussed below.

[3] United States v. Dennis, 183 F.2d 201, 211 (1950), *aff'd,* 341 U.S. 494 (1951).

[4] Dershowitz, *Preemption,* 13; see also John Yoo, *Using Force,* 71 U. Chi. L. Rev. 729 (2004).

the seriousness, likelihood, and moral costs of prevention, or its prospects of success. Drawing on "just war"
theory and other sources, I now turn to these issues.

Four Standards

Standards for prevention should look beyond imminence and active preparations to four wider considerations of *lethality, likelihood, legitimacy,* and *legality* in
order to assess the seriousness of threats not yet imminent and the appropriate responses to them.[5]

- *Lethality* identifies the likely loss of life if the threat is
  not eliminated.
- *Likelihood* assesses the probability that the threat will
  occur.
- *Legitimacy* covers the traditional just war criteria of
  proportionality, necessity, and deliberativeness of proposed responses.
- *Legality* asks whether the threatening situation is itself
  produced by legal or illegal actions, and whether the
  proposed remedy is more or less legal.

Building on just war theory, I argue that all four standards are necessary to justify prevention. Absent good

---

[5] Procedural solutions are necessary complements to any set of substantive standards, if only to reflect the irreducible uncertainty that
will surround nearly all determinations of preventive self-defense. But
I will focus my attention on substantive standards, mostly because
procedural standards are covered by established law and addressed
persuasively (to me) in current scholarship. See, e.g., Tom Farer, "A
Paradigm of Legitimate Intervention," in *Enforcing Restraint*, 316–
47; Buchanan and Keohane, "The Preventive Use of Force"; and
Bjola, "Legitimating the Use of Force in International Politics."

reasons relevant to each standard, preventive action is not justified. The first two *L*'s track existing standards for threat assessment implicit in the Bush Doctrine.[6] Legitimacy, the third, is often a critical hurdle to justification of action, even when the threat is serious. Legality, the fourth, is, I think, distinctive to this approach to preventive enforcement.[7] It should shape both threat assessment and the range of permissible, proportionate responses.

Lethality

The first standard, *lethality,* is conceptually straightforward. It measures the amount of anticipated harm, including the lives or other things of value, such as territorial integrity or political independence, that would be lost, discounted by the reversibility of the harm. Obviously, lives lost are irreversible; property damage may be reversible. But not all property damage is equally reversible. For instance, the destruction of Jerusalem, Mecca, Angkor Wat, Kyoto, Westminster, the Vatican, or the U.S. Capitol has greater significance than the destruction of

[6] See, e.g., Yoo, *Using Force,* and Dershowitz, *Preemption,* and sources cited therein.

[7] President A. Barak of the Israeli Supreme Court in his judgment in the *Targeted Killings Case* avoids blanket rules and, drawing on human rights norms, develops a similar mix of case law standards including proportionality (legitimacy), accuracy (likelihood), and ex post independent investigation (legality) to decide when a targeted killing would be legitimate in an ongoing (*jus in bello*) war (http://elyon1.court.gov.il/Files_ENG/02/690/007/a34/02007690.a3 11/26/2007). Abraham Sofaer discusses related concepts and raises the importance of Charter principles. Below I expand this with a wider consideration of legality both of the target and of the agents claim-

other, less culturally meaningful pieces of real estate.[8] In addition, the capacity to inflict widespread damage has greatly increased. Nuclear, biological, and chemical weapons have created new dimensions of destruction.

Likelihood

The second standard, *likelihood,* is more complicated. In international relations theory, two broad patterns of thought—realism and liberalism—attempt to predict the likelihood of the aggressive use of force in the international system.[9]

Thomas Hobbes, the great seventeenth-century philosopher of political realism, explained how insecurity and anticipation were linked: "And from this diffidence of one another, there is no way for any man to secure himself, so reasonable, as anticipation; that is, by force, or wiles, to master the persons of all men he can, so long, till he see no other power great enough to endan-

---

ing self-defense. See Abraham Sofaer, *On the Necessity of Preemption,* 14 Eur. J. Int'l L. 209 (2003).

[8] Reflecting this kind of calculation, Secretary Stimson removed Kyoto from the target list of the atomic bombs that would destroy Hiroshima and Nagasaki. See Henry Stimson and McGeorge Bundy, *On Active Service in Peace and War* (New York: Harper & Bros., 1947), 612–33.

[9] In Michael Doyle, *Ways of War and Peace* (New York: Norton, 1997), I survey and evaluate realist, liberal, and socialist theories, including Thucydides, Hobbes, and Kant. For Hobbes and Kant, see also Richard Tuck, *The Rights of War and Peace: Political Thought*

ger him: and this is no more than his own conservation requireth, and is generally allowed."[10] Realism holds that relative *capabilities* are the best indicator of threat. This view is identified with the writings of philosophers from fifth-century BCE Athenian general Thucydides to contemporary conservative thinkers Henry Kissinger and—at least before she became President Bush's national security adviser—Condoleezza Rice.

Realists argue that states are basically similar, self-interested actors. They are driven by the competition for material goods, contests over prestige, and fear of being conquered. The first motive leads to war when one state is considerably stronger and does not expect costly resistance to its predation; the second and third when power is more or less equal as neither state is likely to defer to the prestige of the other, or to know whether its power is sufficient to deter the other from attacking. Given the likely uncertainty about another state's motivation, rational states rarely experience security. They may clash even when each thinks it is seeking security but, absent a Global Leviathan, has no sure way to know whether the security of other states is compatible with its own. War, then, is an ever-present possibility in the international system.

War becomes especially likely when power relations are changing, when formerly weaker states are catching up to formerly stronger states, who are then tempted to

and the International Order from Grotius to Kant (Oxford: Oxford University Press, 1999), 126–39, 207–25.

[10] Thomas Hobbes, *Leviathan*, bk. 13, ed. Richard Tuck (Cambridge: Cambridge University Press, 1996), 99.

prevent equality through preventive war. Thus, according to Thucydides in *The Peloponnesian War,* "what made war inevitable was the growth of Athenian power and the fear which this caused in Sparta."[11]

Liberalism, on the other hand, focuses on institutionalized *intentions.* The eighteenth-century German philosopher Immanuel Kant argued that liberal republics could establish a self-sustaining peace amongst themselves,[12] which contemporary theorists call the "democratic peace."[13] Although states throughout history have gone to war with each other to advance both their national and governmental interests, liberal democratic peoples have, by and large, respected each other's sovereignty and security. Liberal democratic republics do not wage war against each other, although they do against nondemocratic states. The theory behind "democratic peace" is that liberal republics are responsible to the majority of electors, who, unlike monarchs and dictators, cannot regularly displace the costs of going to war on others. If, moreover, those electors embrace liberal principles, they will respect the rights of peoples similarly free to express their rights, and negotiate rather than fight over differences of interest. Respect for property

[11] Thucydides, *The Peloponnesian War,* bk. 1, ch. 1, trans. David Grene (Chicago: University of Chicago Press, 1989).

[12] See Immanuel Kant, "Eternal Peace," in *The Philosophy of Kant: Immanuel Kant's Moral and Political Writings,* ed. Carl J. Friedrich (New York: Modern Library, 1949), 430.

[13] See, e.g., *Debating the Democratic Peace,* ed. Michael E. Brown, Sean M. Lynn-Jones, and Steven E. Miller (Cambridge, MA: MIT Press, 1996).

rights and the benefits of commercial exchange reinforce these moral commitments. Therefore, liberals assume that liberal republics will not threaten each other. At the same time, however, republics will be threatened by—and will therefore threaten—dictatorships because dictatorships do not exercise representative restraint, lack principled respect for human rights, and do not benefit from the same unfettered commercial exchanges.

Contemporary liberal scholars Lee Feinstein and Anne-Marie Slaughter have modernized these preventive arguments with respect to the dangers articulated by President Bush.[14] Feinstein and Slaughter propose that dictatorships armed with weapons of mass destruction should be regarded as sufficiently dangerous that—with proportionality considerations also taken into account and with a preference for multilateral solutions—a preventive attack against them would be justified. The lack of constitutional safeguards in dictatorial states and the extreme dangers of weapons of mass destruction provide the persuasive core of Feinstein and Slaughter's argument.

Both realist and liberal theories have their strengths in fleshing out the *likelihood* standard. But neither—despite their frequent use in arguments about preventive

---

[14] Lee Feinstein and Anne-Marie Slaughter, "A Duty to Prevent," *Foreign Affairs* 83, no. 1 (2004): 136–50. For a good pre-9/11 account of how technology is stressing traditional standards that supports Feinstein and Slaughter's argument, see Michael N. Schmitt, *Bellum Americanum: The U.S. View of Twenty-First Century War and Its Possible Implications for the Law of Armed Conflict,* 19 Mich. J. Int'l L. 1051 (1998).

self-defense—is a sufficiently reliable guide to a substantive standard to guide preventive action. The problem is that both are overinclusive.[15] For example, the realists would have predicted conflict when the United States surpassed British power (potential) in the early 1900s.[16] Yet the two liberal powers maintained peace. For their part, the liberals fail to consider that while dictatorships may not be part of the liberal peace, wars are nonetheless rare events and the typical dictatorship rarely provokes a war.[17]

Of course, dictatorships sometimes do launch aggres-

---

[15] For a good survey of the empirical record, see Jack S. Levy, "Declining Power and the Preventive Motivation for War," *World Politics* 40, no. 1 (1987): 82–107.

[16] As early as the 1830s Alexis de Tocqueville predicted in *Democracy in America* that the two superpowers of the twentieth century would be the United States and Russia. See Alexis de Tocqueville, *Democracy in America,* trans. Henry Reeve (New York: Adlard and Saunders, 1838; reprint, Clark, NJ: Lawbook Exchange, 2003), 414. Explaining why, from a purely power potential point of view, the British Empire aligned with the United States against Germany rather than with Germany against the United States has thus become a conundrum. See Niall Ferguson, "The Kaiser's European Union," in *Virtual History: Alternatives and Counterfactuals,* ed. Niall Ferguson (London: Papermac, 1998), 228, 239: "*A priori,* there is no obvious reason why an 'overstretched' power (as Britain perceived itself to be) and an 'under-stretched' power (as Germany perceived itself to be) should not have cooperated together comfortably on the international stage." See also Niall Ferguson, *The Pity of War* (London: Penguin Press, 1998), 45–55, 68–76.

[17] The classic in this literature is Stanislav Andreski, "On the Peaceful Disposition of Military Dictatorships," *Journal of Strategic Studies* 3, no. 1 (1980): 3–10.

sive wars, when they fear getting weaker (e.g., Japan against the United States in December 1941) or seek to capitalize on their strength before it erodes (e.g., Germany in 1939–41). Liberal states also launch aggressive wars, sometimes to rescue vulnerable populations, sometimes to protect their own citizens or property, and sometimes simply because they are mistaken in their assessment of threats to their security. Adopted wholesale, therefore, either the realist or the liberal theory of likelihood would lead to far too many false positives (preventive wars against threats that would not have materialized) and may even produce false negatives (missed threats that caught the victim by surprise).

Practical assessments of likelihood must therefore reflect a more complex algorithm, including announced threats and past aggressive behavior, in addition to power, ideologies, and regime characteristics. As I mentioned in my first essay, Michael Walzer has argued for going beyond imminence as the standard for preemption, using as an example the Six-Day War between Israel and Egypt in 1967. There he highlighted manifest intent to injure (e.g., Egyptian nonrecognition of Israel and Egypt's closing of the Straits of Tiran to Israeli shipping); active preparations (e.g., Egypt mobilizing forces on Israel's border); and increasing danger (e.g., the unsustainable costs of Israel's mobilization of its reserve forces). The last factor was decisive. There is evidence that while Israel appears to have been aware that Nasser may well have been bluffing, Egypt's bluff imposed an intolerable burden on Israeli security. Israel could not call the bluff by standing down without making itself vulnerable to an attack. Thus lethality, the pattern of threats, and necessity dominated.[18]

Even more preventively—that is, less imminently—is Emmerich de Vattel, the great eighteenth-century jurist. In his *Law of Nations* (1758), he proposed that preventive war could be justified when an opponent has demonstrated clear signs of "rapacity," acquires a formidable augmentation of power, and then, when asked, fails to provide peaceful assurances and guarantees.[19] Just as Walzer drew his principles from the experience of the Six-Day War, Vattel reflected on the origins of the War of the Spanish Succession (1701–14) when European powers joined together to prevent the dangerous acquisition of Spain by Louis XIV's grandson, who could then have inherited both thrones.[20]

But even announced threats and manifest intent have their limitations as reliable signals. Some open threats are bluster or ambiguous (e.g., Khrushchev's Cold War "we will bury you"—by which, he later said, he meant to announce that the USSR would outcompete the United States in industrial production). And some threats are designed to be hidden in order to facilitate surprise (e.g., Pearl Harbor).

In assessing likelihood, I will therefore borrow from each line of thought. From liberalism I will discount the potential threat of liberal regimes (to other liberals). From realism, I will focus on when overall capacity and technical feasibility of the threat are increasing (e.g., nu-

---

[18] Walzer, *Just and Unjust Wars*, 82–85.

[19] Vattel, *The Law of Nations*, bk. 3, 44, 308.

[20] See ibid.

clear proliferation). And from manifest behavioral patterns, I will focus on explicit threats, patterns of aggressive behavior, and failures to give credible guarantees. Assessing the likelihood of threats should reflect all three.

The key distinction between preemption and prevention is captured by likelihood. Preemption is motivated by wars that are expected to occur imminently; prevention by wars that, if they must be fought, are better fought now than later. Certainty and uncertainty are what connects them. The traditional imminence standard of preemption justifies action because the threat, other things equal, is more likely to be realized when it is proximate than threats that are less imminent, simply because the evidence of more remote threats will be less clear and time may solve the problem (aggressive leaders die). The likelihood of less imminent threats that justify preventive action is shaped by a change in military capabilities that produces a significant rise in threatening power, a change in regime that produces a significant shift in expected intentions, or a change in an actor's behavior; each may trigger a justifiable preventive war if the threats are sufficiently certain and large.[21]

[21] Here my argument is closer to the analysis of prevention in Gaddis, *Surprise, Security, and the American Experience,* and Trachtenberg, "Preventive War and U.S. Foreign Policy," than to the valuable paper by Jack S. Levy, who focuses on changes in military capabilities in "Preventive War and the Bush Doctrine: Theoretical Logic and Historical Roots," in *Understanding the Bush Doctrine: Psychology and Strategy in an Age of Terrorism,* ed. Stanley A. Renshon and Peter Suedfeld (New York: Routledge, 2007). While Levy seeks to narrow the concept of prevention in order to analyze the policy effects of changes in relative capabilities, my aim is to consider the

This logic clearly applies to states. But so-called asymmetric threats from nonstate actors—namely, terrorists—raise more troubling considerations when it comes to likelihood. When before in human history have so few private individuals armed with such simple weapons (box cutters) been able to kill so many people as quickly as they did on 9/11? Private groups choosing terrorist tactics become exponentially more dangerous for reasons discussed above and because one cannot assume them ever to be at "peace." Their affiliation with campaigns of terror itself is like a declaration of war; like their antecedents, the pirates, such groups can be assumed to be *hostes humani generis*, "at war with humankind."[22] Thus when an individual joins such a group that has engaged in a clear record of terrorist attacks, he or she can be regarded as inherently dangerous and made subject to surveillance and, if the circumstances warrant, detention, prosecution, and defensive use of preventive force (with all the appropriate Geneva Conventions and relevant domestic constitutional protections).[23]

---

full breadth of circumstances in which preventive action would be ethically justified. For example, in the unlikely event that Canada was threatened by a military coup, this would constitute a step-level increase in threat to the United States justifying proportional measures to prevent the coup, even though no increase in Canadian military capabilities was evident.

[22] For discussion, see *U.S. v. Smith,* 18 U.S. (5 Wheat.) 153 (1820); and Hugo Grotius, *The Rights of War and Peace,* bk. 3, ch. 3, 1, ed. Richard Tuck (Indianapolis, IN: Liberty Fund, 2005), 1246–47.

[23] For a discussion on how to do this, see Bruce Ackerman, *Before*

Legitimacy

The third standard, *legitimacy,* itself includes three elements: (1) weighing proportionately the threatened harm against the likely benefit-cost of the response; (2) limiting the response to the minimum necessary to effectively deal with the threat; and (3) seeking the relevant deliberation.

Proportionality and necessity do an immense amount of work in determining the legitimacy of preventive force.[24] A countermeasure must make strategic sense if it is to be justified. There must be a military advantage to striking first rather than waiting.[25] Beyond that, striking first calls for ethical justification. Conventional responses to large threats—blockades (or mandatory sanctions), surgical strikes, and all-out military interventions—all break the laws of peacetime international

---

the Next Attack: Preserving Civil Liberties in an Age of Terrorism (New Haven: Yale University Press, 2006). See also notes 73 and 74 below for other important considerations.

[24] See UN Secretary-General, *Report of the High-level Panel on Threats, Challenges and Change,* 63–67, which also builds upon classic just war doctrine and the authority of eminent statespersons, such as former National Security Adviser Brent Scowcroft, to defend similar legitimacy standards. The standards I defend here pay more attention to legality as a signal and standard, and also do not limit justified action to Security Council approval.

[25] For a good discussion of those circumstances, see Karl P. Mueller et al., *Striking First: Preemptive and Preventive Attack in U.S. National Security Policy* (Santa Monica, CA: RAND Project Air Force, 2006), especially chap. 2, pp. 19–42.

relations and thereby require justification as defensive measures. But they clearly have different effects. In international law, violations of sovereign rights are all the same in their illegality.[26] But in practice, a blockade or mandatory multilateral sanctions leave more political independence and territorial integrity intact than a targeted, "surgical" military strike. Similarly, a military strike is less violative than an invasion and occupation.

Discriminating between combatants and noncombatants is an essential feature of just war doctrine. It is especially important for preventive measures to be even more discriminating, targeted on those most responsible for the threat, given the greater uncertainties involved. We must consider the possibility that some threats might be secret even from the soldiers who might someday implement them.[27] The specific calculation needs to be made on a case-by-case basis, partly because probable casualties differ, and not always in a symmetric, similar fashion. The loss of life indirectly attributable to sanctions in Iraq after 1991 was much greater than the loss of life in the surgical strike against Osirak in 1981. And some threats may be addressable only through invasion and occupation. Occupation was necessary to address the Nazi threat to the future of Europe in 1945, after its armies had been pushed back to the German frontiers; so, too, rooting out al Qaeda in Afghanistan probably required defeating the Taliban by invading

[26] The classic case is Corfu Channel (Merits) (U.K. v. Alb.), 1949 I.C.J. 4 (Apr. 9), which held that sovereign independence was integral and indefeasible.

[27] I owe the secrecy point to a comment made by Jeff McMahan.

Afghanistan. The calculus shows up best in specific cases, as I will later demonstrate.

Necessity also means necessary now, rather than later. This is not the same as *Caroline*-ian imminence, but it does mean that reasons need to be given as to why, if no action is taken now, the threat will materialize and be more difficult to meet in the future. Time often resolves threats. For example, the deaths of Mao Tse-tung and Joseph Stalin reduced Cold War threats.

Deliberation, the third element, is important for two reasons. First, decisions to use preventive force encompass inherently uncertain predictions about the future. Including many diverse voices in the decision reduces the effects of "groupthink," premature closure, and political exploitation (i.e., warmongering for political advantage). Second, multilateral deliberation and authorization place the decision within the framework of existing law, to which I now turn.

Legality

The fourth standard is *legality,* or, more precisely, compliance with international law. This standard is more restrictive than existing preventive standards. It asks whether the target regime has violated international law, in either its domestic actions (e.g., egregious human rights violations) or its international behavior, that is, through a pattern of aggression or in its acquisition of threatening capabilities (e.g., acquiring nuclear weapons in violation of the Non-Proliferation Treaty or

IAEA standards). Some violations of international law are so extreme that they require other states to disregard the prohibition on the use of force. Obviously, international aggression or the threat thereof requires the Security Council to act. But so do some "domestic" violations, such as genocide.[28]

The assumption is that neither the nature of the regime (i.e., democracy or dictatorship) nor its power is the crucial determinant; rather, the more illegal the past behavior, by any kind of state, the greater the reliability of the signal of hostile intent. Law is also one step less subjective than presidential perception. It is intersubjective, determined by multilateral agreement or long customary practice.

In addition to the legality of the target regime's actions, this standard also focuses on the legality of the preventive response. Some infringements on sovereignty—for instance, on political independence and territorial integrity—are worse than others. Proportionality in response to an actual armed attack is not required, but rather may be gauged to address the overall threat to territorial integrity and political independence (where *jus in bello* standards still apply). In contrast, proportionality should be more strictly applied in preventive actions.[29] Greater uncertainty, which is

[28] The Genocide Convention requires all states "to prevent and to punish" the crime of genocide. See "Convention on the Prevention and Punishment of the Crime of Genocide," December 9, 1948, *United States Statutes at Large* 102:3045, art. 2 (entered into force January 12, 1951).

[29] Usefully distinguishing the *Caroline* where the United States

equivalent to lesser imminence, justifies this safeguard. A more legal response is also more likely to garner multilateral authorization with the ancillary benefits of greater burden sharing and wider legitimacy. Most important, and as noted above, multilateral authorization is the single best way to reduce the risk of self-interested interpretation in which states invent or exaggerate convenient threats in order to pursue other interests, international and domestic.

1. Multilateral authorization through the Security Council should therefore be the first resort of preventive self-defense. No state should resort to regional authorization or unilateral action unless this remedy has been exhausted.

2. Each of the members of the council should state in public in the council its reasons for accepting or rejecting the application to authorize prevention. If the arguments I am presenting here are persuasive, these reasons should be articulated as answers to the four standards. Indeed, one of the key reasons to develop standards is to enhance the quality of the deliberation that these difficult decisions should launch. These decisions should engage both the citizens of the state proposing to prevent and the international community more broadly, both officially in the Security Council and unofficially in the global media.

---

was not an aggressor (but was failing to govern its borders) from active aggressive intent, Timothy Kearley suggested that proportional response to the attack should not be strictly measured in genuine preemptive defense when the threatening state itself intends the harm. See Kearley, *Raising the Caroline*.

But, given the veto possessed by the superpowers and the less-than-perfect reliability of any procedural standard, including the Security Council vote, the UN cannot be the only resort for preventive self-defense; some unilateral acts must be permitted. The mere fact that unilateral action could be considered legitimate should have a responsibility-inducing effect on the Security Council. Rather than enjoying a monopoly, the council will now know that its actions are subject to the "market" of alternative judgment. But when unilateral preventive measures do take place, two additional accountability mechanisms should be set in motion to assess domestic and international legitimacy.

3. A national commission should examine the facts of the matter and issue a public report.[30]

4. Lastly, that report should be submitted to the Security Council. The council should then launch an international investigation of the justifiability of the action and prepare a report (subject to a majority vote, not subject to vetoes).[31]

---

[30] I owe the suggestion of a national commission to Bob Keohane. He and Allen Buchanan recommend an impartial international commission to assess damages ex post on states wrongly claiming prevention or wrongly voting against justified claims to use preventive force, "The Preventive Use of Force."

[31] This parallels Barak's suggestion in *Targeted Killings*; see p. 47, n. 7, above. In extreme circumstances, the UN Security Council report might serve as the preliminary evidentiary basis for a decision to prosecute by the International Criminal Court (either because war crimes violations have taken place or, when once defined, aggressive war has occurred). These judgments would be made at the discretion of the prosecutor and the panels to which he or she would present

The overall set of standards that I propose is systemic; each is necessary and all are interrelated. We can think of them as multiplicative not additive:

$$\text{Justified Prevention} = \text{Lethality} \times \text{Likelihood} \\ \times \text{Legitimacy} \times \text{Legality}$$

That is, if one standard measures in at zero, no preventive action is justified. Combined, they provide guidelines for determining when prevention is justified. First, if a threat is not imminent, and hence uncertain, it can still be likely enough that, when the lethality is taken into account, it is as dangerous as a threat justifiably preempted. Correlatively, justified preventions thus usually involve much greater lethality than justified preemptions and much less costly responses; typically, sanctions rather than invasions. Second, acquisitions of destructive capabilities by law-abiding states, whatever their ideology, should not be considered sufficient evidence to justify preventive measures. Third, the greater the lethality and likelihood of an attack by a threatening regime, the less egregious its violations of international law must be in order to justify prevention. And, as a corollary to this, the less concern about legality should restrict the Security Council's or victim state's response. And fourth, flipping the second consideration, the less the lethality and likelihood of the threatened attack, the greater the weight that should be placed on both the legality of the threatening regime's actions and any potential international response.

---

evidence. See Rome Statute of the International Criminal Court, A/CONF.183/9*, entered into force July 1, 2002.

To demonstrate how these guidelines could operate in practice, I now turn to several contentious cases involving the use of preventive force.[32]

Difficult Cases

The first set of cases illustrates the significance of the sliding scale. Here, I plan to discuss three important but hard cases: (1) the standards the Security Council employed in its fully legal imposition of mandatory sanctions on South Africa in response to South Africa's regime of apartheid; (2) the Cuban Missile Crisis of 1962 and the subsequent imposition of a "quarantine" by the United States; and (3) the Israeli attack on Iraq's Osirak nuclear reactor in 1981. I will conclude with briefer remarks on counterterrorism efforts, the U.S. invasion of Iraq in March 2003, and the current crisis with Iran over its nuclear program (civilian or military?).

Multilateral Cases: South African Apartheid, 1977

The distinguishing features of prevention mandated by the Security Council are legality and procedural legiti-

---

[32] In looking at cases in this way to discover and test standards for the use of force, I follow the related methods used, to explore reprisals, by Richard Falk in *The Beirut Raid and the International Law of Retaliation*, 63 Am. J. Int'l L. 415–43 (1969) and Derek Bowett *Reprisals Involving Recourse to Armed Force*, 66 Am. J. Int'l L. 1–36 (1972).

macy. Current international law grants wide discretion to Security Council decisions when it is acting under Chapter VII. The council, moreover, is widely representative of the international community and is its designated agent for preserving international peace and security.[33] As discussed in my first essay, all UN member states, large and small, gave the council this role when they negotiated and signed or acceded to the UN Charter. The council is neither a court of law nor a legislature, but its decisions are binding. They incorporate interested calculations of states (and the potential vetoes of the Permanent Five) and should evince a respect for international law, forming a particularly significant source of evolving customary international law. The standards that the Charter explicitly or implicitly employs in its "jurisprudence" of prevention are thus worth our attention.

The other distinctive feature of this preventive jurisprudence is a strong disinclination to draw hard and fast lines between domestic and international threats, despite the fact that the council's jurisdiction is defined as threats to "international" peace and security. The council, confronted with the actual connections between the two, regularly identifies both and draws the

---

[33] For thorough discussions of the legality and procedural legitimacy of the Security Council's imposition of sanctions against Libya, see Ian Hurd, *After Anarchy: Legitimacy and Power in the United Nations Security Council* (Princeton: Princeton University Press, 2007), and Erik Voeten, "The Political Origins of the Security Council's Ability to Legitimize the Use of Force," *International Organization* 59, no. 3 (2005): 527–58.

implicit connection. International threats clearly qualify, as they did when the council condemned violations of the Palestine cease-fire and the North Korean attack on South Korea (though in the latter instance it expanded "international" to include what some alleged to be a civil war). However, domestic violations of human rights abuses alone do not rise to the level of international threat. For example, in 1946 the council rejected Poland's call for the imposition of sanctions on fascist Spain, after finding that its domestic abuses did not engender threats to its neighbors.[34]

In the Rhodesian and South African cases, however, the Security Council clearly connected the two. Under Resolution 232 (1966), the council imposed Chapter VII trade sanctions against the racial minority regime of Ian Smith in Rhodesia when it unilaterally seceded from the United Kingdom. But the South African case most clearly illustrated the new jurisprudence of prevention. Resolution 418 (1977) condemned the South African government for, in the following order: (1) "massive violence against and killing of the African people, including school children and others opposing racial discrimination"; (2) "*apartheid* and racial discrimination" (whose elimination the resolution demanded); (3) the "military build-up" and "persistent acts of aggression against neighbouring States"; and (4) the government's "move to the threshold of producing nuclear weapons." Specifically invoking Chapter VII, the council then decided

---

[34] The issue was tabled after the UN Security Council subcommittee came to that conclusion. See David Lowther Johnson, *Sanctions and South Africa*, 19 Harv. Int'l L.J. 887, 892 (1978).

that the acquisition of arms and related matériel "constitute[d] a threat to the maintenance of international peace and security," and imposed a mandatory embargo, equivalent to a blockade.

In assessing *lethal threat* and *likelihood,* the council could have focused solely on South Africa's persistent pattern of violating Security Council resolutions concerning Rhodesia and Namibia or on South Africa's repeated cross-border raids on its neighboring states.[35] Instead, the council linked the South African government's domestic oppression to its international behavior and referenced both as constituting a lethal and likely continuing threat to international peace. Undoubtedly, this choice reflected the widespread anger against apartheid felt by South Africa's African neighbors and the widespread condemnation of South Africa for consequent human rights violations. It also probably reflected, however, a sense of their inherent connection. Defending and extending apartheid is what made South Africa a likely threat to its neighbors and its neighbors dangerous to it. Serious domestic oppression rightly engenders a threatening response from neighbors who refuse to tolerate the abuse of fellow human beings, and who are forced to accept refugees fleeing a well-founded fear of persecution. The council would not have been satisfied simply with a cessation of cross-border raids; it specifically called for the elimination of apartheid.[36]

[35] This record is thoroughly documented in ibid., 917–20.

[36] Yet, previously, the Security Council had refused to invoke Chapter VII to condemn apartheid when it saw apartheid as a purely domestic oppression. See the discussion of Article 39 in Leland M.

The imposition of mandatory sanctions was clearly a *legitimate,* minimal, less than proportional, and in the short run insufficient means to address the threat. But invading South Africa in order to impose a regime change was clearly off the table in the middle of the Cold War and most likely disproportionate in view of South Africa's ability to defend itself. The sanctions were minimal responses to the lethality that apartheid and its continuation posed to South Africa's neighbors—a continuing and likely further threat. Apartheid was a significant violation of human rights, and the sanctions were fully *legal* responses, authorized by the Security Council. In the end, the sanctions, the unilateral embargoes and sanctions they later legitimated, and the widespread condemnation they fostered seem to have strengthened apartheid's opponents and embarrassed its defenders, opening the door to peaceful democratization under Presidents de Klerk and Mandela.

This linking of domestic and international threats to international peace became a hallmark of Security Council jurisprudence. Threats to the peace included both purely international threats and, increasingly, domestic oppression with international dimensions. Security Council jurisprudence always had to pass a political test: at least nine out of fifteen votes, absent a veto by one of the Permanent Five. Nonetheless, a normative pattern has emerged linking dangerous regimes, dangerous situ-

---

Goodrich, Edvard Hambro, and Anne Patricia Simons, *Charter of the United Nations: Commentary and Documents,* 3rd and rev. ed. (New York: Columbia University Press, 1969), 296–97.

ations, and humanitarian protection to threats to international peace and security. The connection is both legally required—Article 39 requires a determination of an "international threat"—and also substantively elaborated in the resolutions. In the 1990s, this preventive jurisprudence condemned genocide, "ethnic cleansing," and war crimes (Former Republic of Yugoslavia, Iraq, Liberia); interference with the delivery of humanitarian supplies and violations of cease-fires in civil wars (Former Republic of Yugoslavia, Iraq, Somalia); collapse of civil order (Liberia and Somalia); and coups against democratic governance (Haiti).[37] In 1999, it condemned the Taliban for failure to prevent terrorism and for not surrendering Osama bin Laden (Resolution 1276), and imposed trade and financial sanctions. Reflecting this broad interpretation of preventive jurisprudence and constructing the specifically humanitarian element of it, the General Assembly in 2005 itself adopted a statement of principles, *The Responsibility to Protect,* acknowledging that when states fail to protect their populations from genocide, war crimes, and other grave abuses, the responsibility transfers to the Security Council.[38]

This broad jurisprudence of threat is well-suited to multilateral deliberation and implementation. The domestic oppression of others is notoriously subject to invidious and self-interested interpretation. Authorizing a full-scale invasion for the purpose of regime change, as

[37] Lori Damrosch details these in her introduction to *Enforcing Restraint,* 12–13.

[38] UN General Assembly, "2005 World Summit Outcome," ¶¶138–40.

occurred in Haiti to restore elected President Aristide, also calls out for multilateral consensus. Fortunately, and despite the horrendous failures in Rwanda and Somalia, the multilateral system has a positive record of facilitating peacebuilding that can reduce the worst forms of tyranny.[39]

Cuban Missile Crisis, October 1962

When should states risk preventive war if they cannot obtain multilateral authorization? The Missiles of October has become an iconic model of Cold War crisis diplomacy. It also became a deeply problematic case of preventive self-defense. I will argue that the "quarantine," which was, in effect, a blockade and thus an act of war, was justifiable. But I will also argue that it is difficult to see how one could justify what gave rise to the crisis or the armed strike that was planned if the quarantine failed.

The most recent scholarly treatment of the crisis aptly describes it as "the most dangerous event in human history."[40] Considering that U.S. and Soviet missile and bomber forces were capable of inflicting hundreds of millions of casualties, and that the two superpowers came close to the brink of conflict, the judgment rings true.

[39] For examples, see Michael W. Doyle and Nicholas Sambanis, *Making War and Building Peace: United Nations Peace Operations* (Princeton: Princeton University Press, 2006).

[40] Don Munton and David A. Welch, *The Cuban Missile Crisis: A Concise History* (New York: Oxford University Press, 2007), 1.

The background to the crisis reveals profound misunderstandings and risky behavior, including the Bay of Pigs invasion of Cuba, supported by the United States, and Khrushchev's saber rattling over Berlin and decision to secretly deploy the missiles to Cuba. The Cold War conflict conditioned the crisis. The first "front" in the Cold War centered on the confrontation between the United States and the USSR, powers that had locked themselves in a warlike contest for influence and survival in which a gain for one appeared to be a loss for the other. The contest was kept "cold" by deterrence, the delicate balance of terror, in which the ability and willingness of the two sides to escalate to nuclear confrontation deterred aggressive moves by either superpower. In the 1950s, Soviet conventional military superiority in Europe was offset by U.S. nuclear superiority and airpower. But this balance was far from static. Soviet successes with Sputnik (1957) and rapid production of missiles set off a "missile gap" scare in the United States that—ironically, as it would turn out—the United States offset by deploying intermediate-range missiles to allies in Europe, including Turkey.[41] Candidate John Kennedy had played upon the "missile gap" to discredit the Republican administration. Once elected and armed with better intelligence, he then revealed in October 1961 that there was a gap; and it massively favored the United States.

[41] The formula pointed out by *Time* magazine was "IRBM + NATO = ICBM," as noted by John Gaddis in his influential reinterpretation of the Cold War, *We Now Know* (Oxford: Oxford University Press, 1997), 264.

The second "front" in the Cold War was the allegiance of the Third World countries, partisans neither of the First (Western, United States) World nor of the Second (Eastern, Soviet) World. Chairman Khrushchev identified this as a region ripe for communist revolution, offering the prospect of tilting the world political balance in favor of the USSR.

Cuba thus brought both fronts together. By deploying thirty-six medium-range ballistic missiles capable of reaching New York and Chicago and twenty-four intermediate-range ballistic missiles capable of reaching all of the lower forty-eight U.S. states and much of Canada and Latin America,[42] the Soviet Union both improved the global nuclear balance and secured the Cuban revolution.

President Kennedy designated an Executive Committee (ExComm) to advise him on a response. They were divided in their assessments and recommendations. Defense Secretary Robert McNamara doubted whether the missiles in Cuba significantly altered the military balance, since the Soviet Union was already capable of striking the United States with nuclear missiles from submarines and from the USSR itself.[43] They also differed on the best response, some favoring an immediate invasion, others a massive air strike or a surgical air strike, and others still a blockade. None favored tolerating the deployment, as the Soviets had been forced to

[42] The USSR also deployed additional forces—land, air, and sea (coastal defense forces)—to protect the missile batteries. See Munton and Welch, *The Cuban Missile Crisis*, 34–37.

[43] Ibid., 52.

tolerate deployments of nuclear missiles in Turkey and Europe. However, Adlai Stevenson, Kennedy's UN ambassador, and McNamara did advocate a trade: missiles in Turkey for missiles in Cuba—the option that the president would at the end select, and keep secret.[44]

Despite their differences, the president and his advisers saw the missiles as posing a significant increase in the *lethality* of the threat to the United States by reducing warning time and targeting (two to three times) more missiles on the United States.[45] It is, however, also fair to say that all were aware of the fact that the administration had pledged to keep missiles out of Cuba and that leaders of the Republican Party were accusing Kennedy of being weak on Cuba. Leaving the missiles in Cuba would expose the administration to serious political losses in the upcoming midterm elections. But the threat they saw was national and not just political.

The deployment of missiles raised the *likelihood* of lethal conflict in four ways.[46] First, the deployment raised questions about who would be in control in a crisis, Castro or Khrushchev. Kennedy made it clear in his

[44] Ibid., 52–53.

[45] Gaddis, *We Now Know,* 268.

[46] Ted Sorensen, interview by author, July 31, 2006. Sorensen focuses on the last three. He adds that if the Soviets had publicly announced the deployment or confidentially informed the United States so that the administration could have prepared the U.S. public, the United States would not have been as concerned. Kennedy would still, however, have had serious domestic political problems if he had chosen to tolerate the missiles. Leonard Meeker also provided helpful insights on this point when I interviewed him on August 14, 2006.

speech announcing the missile threat, on October 22, that any missile launched from Cuba would be regarded as a missile launched by the Soviet Union. Second, most thought it reduced warning time and increased Soviet potential for a fast strike "out of the blue." Third, a risk-prone leader could use such a strike for coercive bargaining, as the United States had used the atomic bombs on Hiroshima and Nagasaki. The missiles could be bargained for assets the United States did not want to lose, such as West Berlin.[47] And, fourth and most important, the secret deployment signaled risky behavior. Ted Sorensen, the president's adviser, has said that the secrecy of the deployment was the key problem, raising fundamental questions of peace and war.[48] In his communiqué to Khrushchev just before he spoke to the nation on October 22, Kennedy stressed deception as the threat and his sense that he had been directly and personally betrayed by the violation of assurances that he thought he had received from Khrushchev at their Vi-

[47] There is no evidence in the Soviet sources that this was part of the plan, but U.S. planners thought that this might be the motivation. The case *for* this argument is in *The Kennedy Tapes: Inside the White House during the Cuban Missile Crisis,* ed. Ernest R. May and Philip D. Zelikow (Cambridge, MA: Belknap Press, Harvard University Press, 1997), and the case *against,* in Munton and Welch, *The Cuban Missile Crisis,* 27.

[48] On numerous occasions before and as late as October 17, following the deployment of the missiles, Khrushchev assured Kennedy through his back channel, Georgi Bolshakov, that "[u]nder no circumstances would surface to surface missiles be sent to Cuba." Munton and Welch, *The Cuban Missile Crisis,* 53.

enna summit in June 1961.[49] Khrushchev's deployment thus seemed to significantly raise the likelihood of Cold War confrontation. Was Khrushchev starting a high-risk confrontation not just in Cuba but throughout the world in order to discredit the United States, intimidate its allies, and dictate a settlement to the Cold War? Were the Soviets rationally deterrable and capable of cooperative detente? And, if not, wouldn't it be better to stop them in the Caribbean, where the United States had so many strategic military advantages?[50]

[49] See Richard Reeves, *President Kennedy: Profile of Power* (New York: Simon & Schuster, 1993), 395, citing "Letter from President John F. Kennedy to Nikita Khrushchev," October 22, 1962, as reprinted in *The Cuban Missile Crisis, 1962: A National Security Archive Documents Reader,* ed. Laurence Chang and Peter Kornbluh (New York: The New Press, 1998), 148–49.

[50] If the main aim of the United States was to restore stable deterrence, once challenged by the USSR, it made sense to stand firm on withdrawal of the missiles and only later, as appropriate, offer concessions to the Soviets (rather than conceding first and later trying to hold the line, a much more difficult strategy to make credible). See the discussion in Glenn Snyder and Paul Diesing, *Conflict among Nations* (Princeton: Princeton University Press, 1977), and Paul Huth, *Standing Your Ground: Territorial Disputes and International Conflict* (Ann Arbor: University of Michigan Press, 1996). Marc Trachtenberg suggests that the uncertainty factor was also significant in explaining the German decision to accept the risks of preventive war with Russia in 1914; it helps explain why, when he was assured that the post-Stalin leadership of the Soviet Union was risk-averse, Eisenhower decided not to try to prevent Soviet nuclear armament. Trachtenberg, "Preventive War and U.S. Foreign Policy," 8–10. For discussions that raised these issues during the crisis, see

The president eventually chose a dual option. First, he authorized a "quarantine," a blockade limited to offensive military equipment, though expandable to cover petroleum if necessary.[51] But he also ordered the air force to be ready, should the quarantine fail, for a full-scale air strike.[52] Fortunately, Khrushchev backed down and ordered the missile deployment to stop. At the same time, and unbeknownst to many of the ExComm, Kennedy opened several secret channels to suggest that he would trade the missiles in Turkey for the missiles in Cuba.

Khrushchev first offered to withdraw the Cuban missiles in return for merely a guarantee that the United States would not invade Cuba, and then in a second communiqué that arrived before the United States could respond to the first, asked for the Turkish missiles as well. Kennedy, in the famous "Trollope Ploy," accepted

---

May and Zelikow, *The Kennedy Tapes,* 91–93, 112–13, 175–77, 229–30.

[51] Leonard Meeker, the deputy legal adviser in the State Department, coined the "quarantine" label and explained the legal case for it. I benefited from an interview with Leonard Meeker by telephone on August 14, 2006. The wider debate in the legal community is reflected in Quincy Wright, *The Cuban Quarantine,* 57 Am. J. Int'l. L. 546 (1963), Myres McDougal, *The Soviet-Cuban Quarantine and Self-Defense,* 57 Am. J. Int'l. L. 597 (1963) and Abram Chayes, *The Cuban Missile Crisis: International Crisis and the Role of Law* (New York: Oxford University Press, 1974). For contemporary citations to this case as "preemptive self defense" see Yoo, *Using Force,* and Wedgwood, *The Fall of Saddam Hussein.*

[52] It is impossible to tell whether this strike would have been executed had Khrushchev refused the secret Turkish exchange Kennedy offered. Kennedy appears to have been ready to accept a public trade

the first offer. Khrushchev then accepted Kennedy's acceptance when Bobby Kennedy, the attorney general and the president's brother, assured Soviet ambassador Anatoly Dobrynin that the missiles would be withdrawn from Turkey provided the deal was kept secret.

The world breathed a collective sigh of relief. The quarantine, though often not presented this way, was a case of justifiable, *legitimate* (though illegal) preventive force. An air strike, however, would not have been justifiable. An air strike would have raised a significant prospect of disproportional escalation to full-scale nuclear war, and disproportionate casualties of hundreds of millions. As it was, the blockade itself was a risky response that was both proportional and sufficient to end the threat.

Regarding *legality,* the Soviet Union had a long record of flagrant aggression, recently repeated against Hungary, though it had done nothing illegal in shipping missiles to Cuba. But given the secrecy and previous assurances that no such deployment would take place, it posed a significant escalation in the likelihood of threatening force. Kennedy appropriately chose the minimum proportional measure that forced the withdrawal of the

---

of the missiles, Turkey for Cuba, that UN Secretary-General U Thant was prepared to propose. But whether a crisis-escalating accident, such as were occurring, would have intervened to upset this second deal is impossible to determine. See discussion in Gaddis, *We Now Know,* 271–74. Silverstone, in his thorough case study of the crisis, concludes that war was inevitable if the Soviets did not remove the missiles: Scott Silverstone, *Preventive War and American Democracy* (New York: Rutledge, 2007), 123.

missiles. He removed a political and strategic threat to the Soviet Union in Turkey in return. He sought multi-lateral legal authorization at the Security Council and presented the U.S. case in full. When the Soviet veto made UN action impossible, he brought the issue to the Organization of American States. Regional organizations cannot legally authorize enforcement measures (Article 53 limits enforcement to the Security Council), but they do offer deliberation and the legitimate authorization that comes from consultation with other states deeply involved in the threatened escalation to war. He also consulted with Macmillan and de Gaulle, key allies in Europe, before announcing the quarantine.

Osirak, June 1981

Israel's surgical strike on Iraq's Osirak nuclear reactor in June 1981 is an example of a unilateral preventive measure that, being one step more aggressive than a block-ade, requires correspondingly stronger justifications. The case has stimulated a thoughtful debate, with Beth Polebaum and Tim McCormack making the case for justified prevention, and Thomas and Sally Mallinson the case against.[53]

[53] Beth Polebaum, *National Self-Defense in International Law: An Emerging Standard for a Nuclear Age*, 59 N.Y.U. L. Rev. 187 (1984). For other views, see Timothy L. H. McCormack, *Self-Defense in International Law: The Israeli Raid on the Iraqi Nuclear Reactor* (New York: St. Martin's Press, 1996), 23–37, 101–10, 211–39, 285–302; and W. Thomas Mallison and Sally V. Mallison,

First, the Iraqi nuclear program was potentially *lethal;* it was both technically feasible and linked to a military purpose. The Osirak reactor was part of a nuclear complex that appeared capable of producing the plutonium that the Israelis believed could provide two or three Hiroshima-sized bombs each year.[54] Roger Richter, a former IAEA inspector, later concluded that the evidence was "numerous, obvious, and compelling" and "[led] to the conclusion that Iraq had embarked on

---

The Israeli Aerial Attack of June 7, 1981, upon the Iraqi Nuclear Reactor: Aggression or Self-Defense?, 15 Vand. J. Transnat'l L. 417 (1982).

[54] The exact status of the Iraqi nuclear program in 1981 still appears uncertain, but a reasonable Israeli official seems to have had grounds for serious suspicion. Adding to the confusion, "Osirak" was one nuclear reactor (Tammuz 1), the smallest one, in a nuclear complex that included a larger reactor (Tammuz 2) and an Italian-built "hot cell" for plutonium extraction. "Osirak" is often used to refer to the whole. Israel probably overestimated the bomb-making capacity of the Osirak complex by a factor of three or four. Physicist Richard Wilson has noted that the Iraqi reactor Osirak was a light-water, not a heavy-water, reactor. Weapons-grade plutonium was a much smaller product of such reactors. See letter to the editor, *Nuclear News,* August 2005. On the other hand, Prime Minister Begin clearly thought that the reactors were heavy-water reactors, like Israel's own reactor at Dimona. What Israeli intelligence believed, however, is not clear. Three additional factors seem to have been important. First, Iraq, when offered lower-enriched fuel from which nuclear bombs could not be made, refused. At U.S. insistence, France then preirradiated the enriched fuel to make bomb extraction more difficult. But Iraq then contracted for the Italian "hot cell" laboratory that could extract plutonium from enriched fuel. See "A Risky Nuclear Game," *Newsweek,* June 22, 1981, 25. Second, Iraq

a nuclear weapons program."[55] One small bomb striking Tel Aviv could kill approximately 100,000 Israeli citizens.[56] The overall pattern of Iraq's nuclear program therefore appeared dangerous enough to warrant concern on the part of Israeli officials.

Second, affecting *likelihood,* was Iraq's manifest intent to use prohibited weapons in war. Saddam Hussein had—even before 1981—a clear record of ruthlessness against foes he thought were vulnerable, including the

---

purchased 250 tons of natural uranium—vastly more than would be needed for a reactor of its size if bomb manufacture were not part of its purpose. And, third, Iraq purchased 10 tons of depleted and natural uranium—ideally suited for plutonium production—and sought to purchase more depleted uranium. See Leonard S. Spector, *Nuclear Proliferation Today* (New York: Vintage Books, 1984); George Amsel, Jean Pierre Pharabod, and Raymond Sene, "Rapport: Osirak et la prolifération des armes atomiques" [Report: Osiraq and the proliferation of nuclear weapons] (Paris: Groupe de Physique des Solides, Université Paris VII, May 1981), reprinted in *Les temps modernes,* September 1981, 375–413; and Jed C. Snyder, "The Road to Osiraq: Baghdad's Quest for the Bomb," *Middle East Journal* 37, no. 4 (1983): 577–78. Unfortunately, IAEA inspections in the 1980s were incapable of detecting subtle cheating. Saddam Hussein greatly increased his investment in nuclear weapons following Osirak's destruction and by 1988 had acquired a significant capability, which was destroyed by the Gulf War aerial attacks and clamped down by the UNSCOM (United Nations Special Commission) inspectors in the early 1990s. See generally McCormack, *Self-Defense in International Law,* 38–61.

[55] Senate Foreign Relations Committee, *The Israeli Air Strike: Hearings before the Senate Committee on Foreign Relations,* 97th Cong., 1st sess., 1981 (statement of Mr. Roger Richter).

[56] Rodger W. Claire, *Raid on the Sun: Inside Israel's Secret Cam-*

domestic opponents of the Baath Party and the Iranians. Beyond that, Israel and Iraq were still technically in a state of war stemming from the concerted attack on Israel in the 1973 Yom Kippur War. But more important than either of those two factors was the explicit link between Saddam's nuclear program and Israel. In addition to their access to various covert sources of information within the Iraqi nuclear program, the Israelis were well aware that the tightly controlled Iraqi press reported Israel's fear of the capacities of an Iraqi nuclear reactor, and that Saddam had asserted that the Arab world must develop nuclear weapons and "destroy Tel Aviv with bombs."[57]

Third, July 1981 was the last available time to act *legitimately,* proportionately. In July, the reactor would come online, and collateral fallout on Baghdad from any attack would make an attack disproportionate. Once the reactor became operational, Israeli intelligence predicted that Iraq would have nuclear bombs by 1985.

Fourth, influencing both *legality* and legitimacy, Israel tried diplomatic, legal alternatives. Prime Minister Begin implored French President Valéry Giscard d'Estaing to pull out the French technicians. Later, Israeli Labor leader Shimon Peres advocated delaying an attack be-

---

paign That Denied Saddam the Bomb (New York: Broadway Books, 2005), 41.

[57] Iraqi News Agency (Baghdad), August 19, 1980; see also discussion in Polebaum, *National Self-Defense in International Law,* 218–19. UNSCOM later found out that in fact Saddam Hussein intended to produce nuclear weapons, but the key issue here is what Israel could reasonably have known at the time. See McCormack, *Self-Defense in International Law,* 45.

cause he thought an attack would accelerate the development of an "Islamic Bomb," and because he believed that the French socialist leader François Mitterand would win the election in France and cancel the sale of nuclear fuel to Iraq. While Mitterand was elected, he did not cancel the sale.[58]

Fifth and finally, again affecting *legitimacy,* Israel proportionally limited its strike to what was needed to end the threat. It destroyed the reactor on a Sunday when Iraqis and foreigners were least likely to be present. Casualties amounted to eight killed, including one French technician.

This does not mean that the Israeli decision to strike the reactor was obvious, easy, or unanimous. The cabinet was initially divided, and defense minister Ezer Weizman resigned in disagreement. The deputy prime minister, Yigal Yadin, required a full briefing by the military authorities and access to the raw intelligence to convince him. In addition, the strike, called Operation Babylon, had a possible domestic political motive (as did the Cuban Missile Crisis). It strengthened Likud and probably helped it win the seats it needed to take full control of the government on June 30, 1981. The UN Security Council in Resolution 487 roundly condemned the attack as an act of aggression, and the United States interposed no veto. The strike may also have accelerated Saddam Hussein's nuclear program.[59] Saddam invested even more in an accelerated program,

[58] Claire, *Raid on the Sun,* 147.
[59] Dan Reiter, "Preventive Attacks against Nuclear Programs and

TABLE 1

Assessments

	Lethality	Likelihood	Legitimacy	Legality[a]	Net Product[b]
South Africa sanctions	S	M	L	SML (M,L)	L
Cuban missiles "quarantine"	L	S	M	S (M,VS)	L
Osirak strike	M	M	M	S (M,VS)	M
Counterterrorism, al Qaeda, 1998	S	L	S	S/M (L,VS)	L
Iraq invasion, 2003	S	M	VS	M (L,S)	VS
"Iran strike, unilateral, 2008"	S	M	VS	S (M,VS)	VS

Note: The assessments here are all impressions based on the history of the events described in the text. VS is "very small," or (if this were quantifiable) bottom quartile of the range of experience on this particular factor, and the measure then ranges to S ("small"), M ("medium"), and L ("large"), or top quartile.

[a] The legality measure is an average of the assessment of the illegality of the target's behavior and the legality of the response. In the parentheses, the first is the illegality of the target; the second is the legality of the response.

[b] The net result is an overall assessment value of the preventive action, the product of lethality × likelihood × legitimacy × legality.

but Iraq was now forced to pursue the much more complicated extraction process using centrifuges and electromagnets, rather than plutonium by-products. In the end, however, despite the greatly increased investment in nuclear weapons production, Saddam did not

the 'Success' at Osiraq," *Nonproliferation Review* 12, no. 2 (2005): 355–71.

have a nuclear bomb before he attacked Kuwait in 1990.[60]

Current Cases

The South African and related multilateral cases illustrate the substantive standards that multilaterally authorized prevention employs. Significantly, the use of force in these cases was authorized by the Security Council and was, therefore, almost ipso facto, legal. The preventive use of force in these cases also deeply intruded on domestic sovereignty in ways that multilateral authorization is more likely to do justifiably.

The unilateral cases are different. Both the Cuban Missile Crisis and the Israeli attack on Osirak illustrate three factors at work: the steep increase in lethal likelihood of the threat to a particular state; the legality of the deployment of the missiles and the development of the reactor, contrasted with the illegality of the threatening regimes' record (primarily their oppressive human rights records); and the necessarily limited character of the response (the quarantine and the surgical strike, respectively).

When we turn to contemporary problems in international security, the four standards help us deliberate about contentious cases. One can wish that the standards generated a sharp set of rules or a precise recipe for judgment and action. But they do not. They are best con-

---

[60] Ibid., 235.

ceived of as a set of relevant questions whose answers in past cases serve as benchmarks for further deliberation.

Counterterrorism Efforts:
Al Qaeda, 1998, and Afghanistan, 2001

On August 7, 1998, car bombs exploded at the U.S. embassies in Dar es Salaam, Tanzania, and Nairobi, Kenya, killing 257 persons and wounding approximately 4,000. On August 20, the Clinton administration fired cruise missiles against an al Qaeda training camp near Khowst in Afghanistan and al-Shifa, a pharmaceutical plant, near Khartoum, Sudan. Osama bin Laden, thought to have planned the two embassy attacks, was said to be at Khowst with a number of top al Qaeda operatives. Al-Shifa was thought to be a nerve gas plant under the control of bin Laden. The attack at Khowst killed 20–30 al Qaeda operatives but unfortunately failed to eliminate bin Laden.

If the Clinton administration's intelligence had been completely reliable, neither attack would have been "preventive." That is, if Osama bin Laden was actually planning future attacks at the Khowst meeting, then the embassy attacks and the fatwa of February 23, 1998, declaring war on the West in general, and the United States in particular, would have constituted an "ongoing" attack within the meaning of the Article 51 definition of self-defense.[61]

[61] Jules Lobel, *The Use of Force to Respond to Terrorist Attacks:*

Some of the intelligence justifying the attacks, however, appears to have been faulty. The administration was not able to produce evidence of nerve gas manufacture in response to the many critics who provided evidence that the al-Shifa plant in Sudan produced pharmaceuticals. Unless we learn more, the al-Shifa attack seems to have been a mistake.

Furthermore, if the Khowst meeting was not a planning meeting for specific attacks, then the U.S. attack was at best justifiable prevention, not self-defense. The administration did apparently have good intelligence that al Qaeda had planned the bombings of the two embassies.[62] Additionally, the fatwa was public knowledge. It was therefore reasonable to assume that al Qaeda had both the intention and the capability (the double explosions in Nairobi and Dar es Salaam were significant demonstrations of this) to attack American citizens again in the foreseeable future, even if not imminently. Having reasonably determined lethality and likelihood, the administration also demonstrated a legitimacy-enhancing concern with proportionality. Before deciding to strike the camps, the planners determined that they were overwhelmingly jihadist encampments and remote from noncombatant Afghan residences.[63]

The Bombing of Sudan and Afghanistan, 24 Yale J. Int'l L. 537, 543 (1999).

[62] National Commission on Terrorist Attacks upon the United States, *The 9/11 Commission Report: Final Report of the National Commission on Terrorist Attacks upon the United States* (New York: Norton, 2004), 115–16 (hereafter cited as *9/11 Report*).

[63] Ibid., 116.

Yet what was missing from the administration's use of force was an attempt to secure a legal basis for the counterterrorist strike. Even if the August 20 intelligence was too time-and-place sensitive to allow for adequate deliberation and a specific authorization in the Security Council, the attacks should subsequently have been deliberated there. Very likely, the United States would have been embarrassed for lack of evidence to sustain the al-Shifa attack, but a case could have been presented against al Qaeda as the Reagan administration publicly presented its case against Libya when it bombed Tripoli in 1986.[64] The outcome is far from certain, but a resolution indicting al Qaeda as a terrorist organization and perhaps even the establishment of a tribunal to try its members would have gone a long way toward legalizing the war against al Qaeda terrorists.

The 1998 attacks missed bin Laden, and no other equivalently good opportunity to prevent al Qaeda's subsequent attacks arose before 9/11.[65] A year after the 1998 attacks, the Clinton administration sought and received UN Security Council condemnation (Resolution 1267) of the attacks and a request backed by (increasingly heavy) sanctions against the Taliban for the extra-

[64] See Reisman, *International Legal Responses to Terrorism,* 31–33.

[65] There were other opportunities, including a potential attack on bin Laden in Kandahar on December 20, 1999, but these potential strikes were based on much less reliable evidence or involved what were thought then to be disproportionate noncombatant casualties. Even the attack on the USS *Cole* lacked a clear fingerprint. *9/11 Report,* 190–97.

dition of Osama bin Laden. The Bush administration continued planning for covert assassinations via Predator drones, but no effective strategy was in place by 9/11. The Taliban continued to provide sanctuary and support for al Qaeda, which in turn continued to finance the Taliban until it was toppled in October 2001 by a U.S.-led coalition acting in self-defense (and in response to the very likely continuing threat of future al Qaeda attacks).[66]

Iraq, 2003

The invasion of Iraq in March 2003 illustrates an unlimited response (invasion and regime change) to Iraq's escalating record of human rights abuse and mixed compliance with Security Council resolutions (more compliance than Saddam Hussein either was prepared to acknowledge or, perhaps, even knew).

Much of the legal debate turned on whether Security

---

[66] Following the 9/11 attacks on the United States and the Taliban's unwillingness to hand over al Qaeda leaders (other than to a sharia court in Afghanistan or Pakistan), the United States and its allies invaded Afghanistan to capture bin Laden and his associates, root out al Qaeda, and topple the Taliban. The action was immediately recognized as an act of self-defense by the UN in Security Council Resolutions 1368 and 1373 on September 12 and 28, 2001, respectively. But again, since there was no evidence that al Qaeda was planning an immediate attack, the justification could just as well have been preventive; bin Laden's past record indicated that as soon as he had the capacity, he would surely strike again.

Council resolutions authorized unilateral enforcement.[67] Proponents cited the numerous resolutions that Saddam had not fully complied with, along with the authorizing language in Resolution 1441 (November 2002). Saddam's failure to comply with the many resolutions requiring him to disarm revived, it is argued, the authorization to use all necessary force embodied in the Gulf War Resolutions 678 (1990) and 687 (1991), and recognized in 1441. Opponents noted the language in 1441 seeming to require a further decision by the Security Council based on information provided to it by UNMOVIC (the UN Monitoring, Verification and Inspection Committee) on the status of Iraq's prohibited weapons. UNMOVIC was not able to make a final determination, and the Security Council did not authorize specific enforcement of 1441.[68]

---

[67] For a balanced assessment of the various positions, see Attorney General Lord Peter Goldsmith, "Memorandum to Prime Minister Tony Blair," March 7, 2003, http://tomjoad.org/goldsmithmemo .pdf. For contemporary debates, see also Yoo, *Using Force,* and Wedgwood, *The Fall of Saddam Hussein.*

[68] This raises important procedural principles. Is the Security Council a legislature, an executive, or a court? The Charter and practice sustain all three interpretations: the council's resolutions are binding and quasi-legislative beyond a particular case; the council makes executive decisions; and the council makes authoritative judgments and imposes penalties based on judgments in particular cases. The safest opinion, and the one most favored by UN legal advisers, is that the council is all three, which means that only the council may interpret its resolutions, and that the council authorizes only what it *explicitly* authorizes. In these respects the closest analogue to the Security Council, oddly, is the old version of the British Privy Council,

Saddam Hussein's record of aggression against his neighbors, and human rights abuses, and failure to cooperate with disarmament verification, provided more than enough evidence to justify a continuation of preventive sanctions and a strengthened regime of inspections. Indeed, one can go further and say that it justified the Desert Fox air attacks of 1998 that were designed to prevent a significant upgrading of the Iraqi air defense system (with Chinese underground communications) that would have made it much more dangerous to enforce the no-fly zones. This was the preventive regime established in 1991 to foreclose Iraq's becoming a power armed with deliverable weapons of mass destruction. It required significant adjustment, to make it less harmful to innocent civilians, but it was working.

In March 2003, however, the lack of evidence that Saddam was successfully developing nuclear weapons or could not be deterred from using chemical or biological weapons against his domestic or international enemies made an invasion and occupation illegitimate, radically

---

which enjoyed a similar breadth of role. One of its subcommittees became the modern cabinet; another the notorious Star Chamber.

[69] Quoted in Bob Woodward, *State of Denial* (New York: Simon & Schuster, 2006), 217.

[70] The existing sanctions regime required revision in order to better target the sanctions at military capacity and the regime, and less at innocent Iraqi civilians. There were more than 200,000 "excess deaths" among children under the age of five between 1991 and 1998 attributable to the sanctions put in place after Saddam Hussein's refusal to disarm. These figures are based on allegations by Denis Halliday, the former UN administrator of the Oil for Food Program who resigned in protest, and on a study by Richard Gar-

disproportionate, and unjustifiable. U.S. intelligence on threat and likelihood was weak. The State Department intelligence office had warned Secretary Powell that the case was far from reliable (far from the "slam dunk" that Director Tenet was claimed to have called it). Prior to his famous February 5 UN speech, Powell weeded the most egregious elements from the draft recommended by the White House. He unfortunately retained specious items including allegations, known in parts of the CIA to be unreliable, of a connection between Saddam Hussein and 9/11 terrorists. David Kay, the Bush administration's final weapons inspector, thought Saddam would be trying to hide WMD, based on his experience as a 1990s UN weapons inspector. But when he surveyed the evidence used by Powell, he concluded, "The more you look at it, the less that is there."[69] Above all, there was no evidence that Saddam was becoming more dangerous, or that the inspections were failing.

The continuing threat that Saddam Hussein posed fully justified the preventive measures the administra-

---

field, "Morbidity and Mortality among Iraqi Children from 1990 through 1998: Assessing the Impact of the Gulf War and Economic Sanctions," July 1999, http://www.casi.org.uk/info/garfield/dr-garfield.html, which was cited by Thomas Pogge in his 2006 Amnesty Lecture, "Making War on Terrorists" (lecture, Oxford University, February 24, 2006). The UN designed an alternative sanctions regime focused on military matériel in the summer of 2001, which culminated in the introduction of a package of reforms (i.e., "smart sanctions") in Security Council Resolution 1409. See Security Council Resolution 1409, S/RES/1409, May 14, 2002. This effort, however, was stillborn in the post-9/11 war on terror.

tion had painstakingly negotiated with the Russians in the spring of 2001. This was a new and more proportional sanctions regime for Iraq, limited to military items that would be monitored at the border.[70] Thus while the legality of the invasion was unclear, the lethality, likelihood, and legitimate proportionality all weighed against an invasion of Iraq in 2003.

"Iran, 2008"

Today, a large-scale preventive attack on Iran, given existing information, would also lack grounds for justification. President Ahmadinejad's threats to "wipe Israel off the map" greatly raise the likelihood of lethal attack. With regard to legality, the threats themselves violate the UN Charter (Article 2.4), and Iran's domestic violations of minority rights create a disturbing pattern. Iranian threats have generated responses, revealing a rising level of threat. Various Israeli officials off the record and Vice President Cheney on the record say: "We join other nations in sending that regime a clear message. We will not allow Iran to have a nuclear weapon."[71]

But Iran's attempts to acquire a nuclear fuel reprocessing capability appear to be within the scope of the Non-Proliferation Treaty. The question is whether Iran is seeking nuclear weapons. The existing level of uncertainty and the likely immense costs of the military action that would be necessary to remove the potential threat

---

[71] Brian Knowlton, "Bush Takes Tough Line, As Does Iran Leader," *International Herald Tribune*, April 18, 2006, 1.

both argue for cautious steps, multilateral authorization, and an initiative limited to sanctions targeted narrowly on military capacity and the governing regime.[72]

A Better Regime against Terrorists

It is fitting to conclude with the acquisition of weapons of mass destruction (WMD) by nonstate actors. This issue profoundly challenges existing international law. International law's conceptions of rights and duties were developed for states and cannot simply be transferred to actors that lack responsibilities for political independence and territorial interests. This is not just because actors such as al Qaeda are more vicious than states (think of Nazi Germany or Stalinist Russia), but because they lack the interests and institutional capabilities that would make them deterrable.

There thus appears to be a strong case for preventive enforcement by the Security Council against any nonstate actor acquiring WMD when its host state fails to take adequate measures. The current structure reflects extensive authority granted by the Security Council in Resolution 1540, but it also reflects two serious gaps. First, multilateral enforcement is inadequate. Reporting on the implementation of Security Council Resolution 1540 prohibitions against the funding, training, and

---

[72] A thoughtful start to this deliberation can be found in Scott Sagan, "How to Keep the Bomb from Iran," *Foreign Affairs* 85, no. 5 (2006): 45–60. See also my response in "Iran and the West: A Symposium," *Dissent,* Winter 2007, 46–47. The U.S. December 2007 National Intelligence Estimate on Iran further compounded the

harboring of terrorists is valuable, but assistance to implement the resolution is thin and enforcement (by whom?) ambiguous. Second, and just as disturbing, is the absence of clear procedures that protect individuals and firms against false accusations of being or supporting terrorists. Innocent persons and organizations may be swept up into its mechanisms and suffer grievous financial and personal harm before an opportunity arises to clear their names. Antiterrorism procedures seemingly mandated by the Security Council could become justifications for rounding up domestic political opponents.[73] Procedures that allow for appeals before publication by the Security Council 1267 (Sanctions) Committee of alleged ties to terrorist groups seem necessary.[74]

---

uncertainty when it announced that Iran had stopped its nuclear weapons program in 2003. But neither the International Atomic Energy Agency nor various European intelligence agencies found the report credible. One French expert described it as "hallucinatory," in John Vinocur, "On Iran, US Policy Implosion Causes Grief for Europe." *Intl. Herald Tribune,* http://www.iht.com/bin/printfriendly .php?id-8669385, 12/11/2007.

[73] Kim Lane Scheppele, "The Migration of Anti-Constitutional Ideas: The Post-9/11 Globalization of Public Law and the International State of Emergency," in *The Migration of Constitutional Ideas,* ed. Sujit Choudhry (Cambridge: Cambridge University Press, 2006), 347–73.

[74] There are currently 359 people on the list. Described as "punishment without trial" by German lawyer Gul Pinar (who represents one of the persons named on the list), UN Security Council procedures allowed no court process before someone is added to the list and no appeal afterward, other than through national processes that might lead the individual's home government to petition to have the individual removed from the list. If an individual's home government used the Security Council Resolution 1267 or 1373 procedures to

Conclusion

Should a responsible government try to deter a potential foe, or should it strike first—that is, preventively—to spare itself from a blow that the other seems to intend, has delivered before, and could again deliver? Is it safer to wait and threaten punishment than to throw the first punch? Or is it wiser to strike now, before the risks increase, even though that means taking the chance that danger might not materialize?

One recourse is for citizens in democracies to trust their elected leaders to identify threats worth attacking preventively. But after Iraq, the American public has become less inclined to back such declarations as President

---

condemn, for example, a dissident, there was no recourse. Named individuals were banned from international travel, had their bank accounts frozen, and suffered other restrictions on economic activity. The Council of Europe has determined that Resolution 1267 procedures do not meet the standards of the European Convention on Human Rights. For a discussion of these issues, see David Crawford, "The Black Hole of a U.N. Blacklist," *Wall Street Journal,* October 2, 2006, A6, and a reply by Ambassador John R. Bolton, letter to the editor, "U.N. Rightly Imposed Sanctions on Terrorists," *Wall Street Journal,* October 6, 2006, A15. See also David Dyzenhaus, "The Rule of (Administrative) Law in International Law," *Law and Contemporary Problems,* 68, nos. 3–4 (2005): 127–66. Two recent developments have improved the rights of those accused of terrorist connections. First, while affirming the nonreviewability of Security Council resolutions other than by *jus cogens* standards (the *Yusuf* and *Kadi* cases), the European Court of First Instance held that Community decisions that interpret and apply Security Council resolutions are reviewable (the *Ayadi* and *Hassan* decisions). It then overturned, on European human rights grounds, the Community regulations implementing Security Council Resolution 1373. Second,

Bush's famous post-9/11 vow not to "wait to be attacked again," to "take the fight to the enemy," and "to defeat them abroad before they attack us at home."

There are no perfectly satisfactory outcomes. The lessons of Hobbesian realism and Kantian liberalism have not been transcended. As long as at least some states lack the accountability and mutual respect of liberal republics, states will lean toward war to resolve fundamental disputes. As long as world politics lacks a world sovereign to resolve disputes, states will engage in self-interested and self-justifying interpretation that will sometimes raise threats, sometimes inadvertently.[75] Imperfect and incomplete as they are, the right decisions about prevention in the world we now live in will rest with democratic publics who understand that their acts will set precedents that others will follow. Answers to questions of lethality, likelihood, legitimacy, and legality are thus far from cure-alls, but they can help publics and the leaders who claim to represent them to do a better job of making careful decisions in matters of life and death.

Security Council Resolution 1730 of December 19, 2006, created a review process that gives individuals a right to submit petitions to, but not participate in, an appeal at the Sanctions Committee. Governments, however, must consent if their nationals are removed from the sanctions list. See European Court of Justice, http://curia.europa .eu/en; Chia Lehnardt, "European Court Rules on UN and EU Terrorist Suspects," *ASIL Insight* 11, no. 1 (2007), http://www.asil.org/ insights/2007/01/insights070131.html.

[75] I found Richard Tuck's remarks on this issue helpful in formulating this point.

COMMENTS

COMMENT

Harold Hongju Koh

In earlier, now-classic scholarly work, Michael Doyle taught us that liberal democracies do not fight with one another.[1] In the same spirit, I am tempted to say that liberal internationalists should not fight with each other. In this comment, I hope to add some lawyerly texture to what I find, overall, is an admirable effort by Doyle to give welcome rigor to a problem that many, most notably the administration of President George W. Bush, have treated with stunning oversimplification.

In his essays in this volume, Michael Doyle claims that if better standards for anticipatory war and warlike measures were codified in international law, better results would follow, including more security for the United States and other states interested in a law-abiding world.

[1] See, e.g., Michael W. Doyle, *Liberalism and World Politics*, 80 Am. Poli. Sci. Rev. 1151 (1986).

As befits his roots in political theory, international relations, and now international law, Doyle treats this claim from three different perspectives: first, just war theory; second, as a liberal international relations theorist who believes in interstate cooperation; and finally as an international lawyer who is advocating a jurisprudence of prevention.

Doyle's case for preventive standards boils down to a simple argument: executive discretion should be channeled by law. He argues that a nation's discretion to use force should be channeled by legal standards, which break into three steps. I will argue that we should respond to Doyle's argument with two cheers: applauding his first two steps, but not his third.

Step One underscores the importance of developing a multilateral framework for sanctioning preventive war. Specifically, he urges that we should channel the Security Council's discretion through legal standards. I find this suggestion altogether welcome.

Step Two calls for channeling and guiding the judgment of the Security Counsel under Article 39 of the United Nations Charter, by developing and following a jurisprudence and case law of anticipatory use of force, a jurisprudence that Doyle illustrates with illuminating examples: Israel's attack on the Iraqi nuclear reactor at Osirak, the Cuban Missile Crisis, and the second Gulf War. Here, I largely agree with him as well.

But where I get off the train is at Step Three, where Doyle says that, in exceptional circumstances, the same legal standards applied to multilateral interventions should also channel the discretion of states, *exercised unilaterally,* to undertake their anticipatory military actions. In practice, I do not believe that "Doyle's Four *L*'s"—lethality, likelihood, legitimacy, and legality—could realistically be expected to guide and limit unilateral military action. Nor do I do think we should encourage their application. My proposal instead would be that we move to a per se ban on unilateral anticipatory war making, with any post hoc justification of such anticipatory actions being asserted as a defense and not in the form of prior permission.

Let me offer five reasons why I believe these two cheers are in order. First, it is simply inappropriate to use the idea of preauthorization for what amounts to a legal defense. You cannot preauthorize a legal defense. Most lawyers are careful to distinguish between defenses and sources of authority to act. Self-defense is a defense. Preemptive use of force is offensive. The notion of "anticipatory self-defense" is therefore an oxymoron, like "defensive offense" or "proactive reaction." To authorize a single nation to make a unilateral action confuses a proactive concept with a reactive concept. For example, lawyers take care not to confuse the necessity defense with prior authorization. If I know that I am not supposed to run a red light and then I see a runaway school bus about to hit a group of schoolchildren, I do not seek prior authority before breaking the law. I do what I believe I am required to do under those highly unusual circumstances, then assert necessity as a defense against subsequent prosecution and conviction. The necessity defense does not serve as a source of prior authority. The necessity defense deals with cases in which an individual must respond to a threat in the context of a particular set of facts, then hopes to argue that under the specific circumstances, with the knowledge available at the time, his or her actions should be viewed as justified in hindsight. This is quite different from furnishing general, prospective criteria to authorize in advance an entire category of actions, as Doyle proposes to do. As former Israeli Chief Justice Aharon Barak put it:

> The "necessity defense" does not constitute a source of authority. . . . The defense deals with cases involving an individual reacting to a given set of facts. . . . [T]he very nature of the defense does not allow it to serve as the source of authorization. Authorization ... is based on establishing general, forward looking criteria rather than defenses to criminal liability.[2]

Doyle's unilateral preemption analysis blurs this distinction between offense and defense, leading to an inevitable slippery slope. After all, if we can attack in preemptive self-defense, there are many other things we can claim to do in self-defense as well. Don't forget that the Justice Department's infamous 2002 Torture Memo said, in effect, that we can torture people in preemptive self-defense.[3] Nor, given that the act ostensibly responded to

[2] Aharon Barak, Israel Supreme Court, *Judgments of the Israel Supreme Court: Fighting Terrorism within the Law* 51–52 (2005) (internal citations omitted), available at http://www.mfa.gov.il/MFA/Government/Law/Legal+Issues+and+Rulings/Fighting+Terrorism+within+the+Law+2-Jan-2005.htm (follow "PDF version (407KB)" hyperlink).

[3] See Memorandum of August 1, 2002, from Jay S. Bybee, Assis-

has not happened yet, is it clear what limit, if any, there is on the range of actions one can take in the name of preemptive self-defense. It is not surprising that the problem of setting limits on how much is enough plagues Alan Dershowitz, who argues both for some forms of preemptive use of force, as well as for some forms of preauthorization of torture in the name of self-defense.[4] So my first point, which I believe constitutes a sufficient objection to Doyle's proposal, is that it is simply a category error to bestow prior legal authorization upon actions that are better addressed in the context of a post hoc defense.

---

tant Attorney General, Office of Legal Counsel, to Alberto R. Gonzales, Counsel to the President, Regarding Standards of Conduct for Interrogation under 18 U.S.C. 2340–40A (August 1, 2004), available at http://news.findlaw.com/nytimes/docs/doj/bybee80102mem .pdf at 45 ("If a [U.S.] government defendant were to harm an enemy combatant during an interrogation in a manner that might arguably violate [criminal law], he would be doing so in order to prevent further attacks on the United States by the al Qaeda terrorist network. . . . This national and international version of the right to self-defense could supplement and bolster the government defendant's individual right.") For analysis and criticism of the Justice Department's Torture Memorandum, see Harold Hongju Koh, *Can the President Be Torturer-in-Chief?*, 81 Ind. L.J. 1145 (2006).

[4] Compare Alan M. Dershowitz, *Why Terrorism Works: Understanding the Threat, Responding to the Challenge* (New Haven: Yale University Press, 2002), 156–63 (supporting an outright ban on torture, but arguing that Congress should pass a statute requiring interrogators to apply to a court for a "torture warrant" that would set limits to the practice), with Alan M. Dershowitz, *Preemption: A Knife That Cuts Both Ways* (New York: W. W. Norton, 2006) (calling, as Doyle does, for a jurisprudence of preemption).

My second objection is that Doyle takes as his model for preauthorization the legal standards governing *multilateral* control of *humanitarian* intervention, as they were developed after the prolonged NATO intervention in Kosovo. In my judgment, however well these multilateral standards governing humanitarian intervention may work, they do not work equally well with regard to *unilateral* uses of preemptive force.

Upon examination, there are at least three critical differences between humanitarian intervention and preemptive intervention. First, in a multilateral situation, there are external, not just internal checks, on the order to use force, and therefore the other countries that are being asked to intervene multilaterally must agree that the standards of humanitarian intervention have been met before the operation can go forward. But if you have worked in the government, you know that unilateral standards are enforced only through unilateral tools. And when the lawyers for a nation think that the nation's very survival is at stake—or if they are pliant or, worse yet, "can-do lawyers" who believe that the president should have unfettered executive power to respond to all crises, real or perceived—then you face a big problem.[5] For if you look at some of the yielding lawyers with whom the current president has surrounded himself, at the White House counsel's office, as attorney general, and as general counsel of the Defense Department,

[5] See, e.g., John Yoo, *The Powers of War and Peace: The Constitution and Foreign Affairs after 9/11* (Chicago: University of Chicago Press, 2005) (arguing for an extraordinarily expansive reading of the president's constitutional authorities over foreign affairs).

COMMENT

you quickly conclude that, sadly, these are not the kind of strong-willed, independent-minded attorneys who, in a unilateral situation, are likely to impose restraints upon the president's will, based on the rule of law.[6]

A second difference between preemptive and humanitarian intervention is that the latter does not, by its nature, breed cycles of counterintervention or cascades of preemption. When NATO engages in humanitarian intervention in Kosovo, that does not cause Serbia to retaliate with humanitarian intervention in Montenegro. As Michael Doyle notes, it is one thing for India to fear Pakistan or for the United States to fear North Korea, but under the current *Caroline* doctrine of self-defense in customary international law, fear alone is not enough. Somebody must make the first move and act in an unambiguously aggressive manner before the object of their aggression can legally respond in self-defense.[7] But if we change the law to authorize a nation to respond,

---

[6] For a journalistic confirmation of this point, see generally Charlie Savage, *Takeover: The Return of the Imperial Presidency and the Subversion of American Democracy* (Boston: Little, Brown and Company, 2007).

[7] In 1837, U.S. Secretary of State Daniel Webster articulated a definition of self-defense that eventually evolved into customary international law, following the famous *Caroline* incident. When British forces destroyed the *Caroline,* a U.S. steamboat attempting to transport supplies to Canadian insurgents, Webster asserted that Britain's actions did not qualify as self-defense, which could be justified only "if the necessity of that self-defense is instant, overwhelming, and leaving no choice of means, and no moment for deliberation." Emanuel Gross, *Thwarting Terrorist Acts by Attacking the Perpetrators or Their Commanders as an Act of Self-Defense:*

not just to a perceived threat, but to a premonition of a perceived threat, or to an inkling of a premonition that your adversary might perceive that you might perceive that he might perceive you as a threat, then, down that hall of mirrors, evidence and proof are quickly replaced by conjecture or assertion. It is not an accident that the perceived need to intervene in Iraq in 2003 to stop Saddam Hussein from using weapons of mass destruction was so widely shared at the time, and has been so widely discredited after the fact.

There is a third, and final, dis-analogy between humanitarian intervention and preemptive intervention. Here I draw upon my experiences as assistant secretary of state during the humanitarian crises in Kosovo and East Timor. When the question of preemption is being seriously considered, there is no meaningful notion of proportional response available. In a humanitarian intervention situation, people are being killed, as was the case in Kosovo and East Timor. That makes it possible to gauge the magnitude of the crisis, and the forces that are perpetrating the war crimes. It becomes possible to estimate how big a force will be needed to intervene, and to map out a long-term strategy for putting an end to conflict, leaving behind a level of forces that will maintain stability on the ground and prevent a new wave of killing from breaking out.

But that is not the case with preemptive self-defense. If you think someone is going to swing at you and per-

Human Rights versus the State's Duty to Protect Its Citizens, 15 Temple Int'l & Comp L. J. 195, 211 (2001).

haps kill you, you have no incentive to calibrate a proportional response. Indeed, if you are sure they plan to kill you, your best bet is to wait until they are sleeping, and then go and kill them first. And that begins to look suspiciously like what some claim motivated the Japanese to undertake the attack on Pearl Harbor. There is no meaningful notion of proportionality that constrains a preemptive attack. To the contrary, the goal of the preemptive attacker is to use maximum force to generate "shock and awe," so that the would-be attacker will quickly capitulate. It is not long before the doctrine leads advocates of preemption to say, "Let's assume necessity," and then to use maximum force, without limitations based on considerations of proportionality.

If you think I am making this up, just recall two memorable maxims of the current administration. First, from Ron Suskind's book *The One Percent Doctrine:* if there is a 1 percent possibility of a serious threat's materializing, you must treat it as a certainty.[8] And the second maxim, a favorite of now-departed Secretary of Defense Donald Rumsfeld: "the absence of evidence is not evidence of absence."[9] In other words, even when there's no smoke, assume there's a fire. When you put these two maxims to-

---

[8] Ron Suskind, *The One Percent Doctrine: Deep Inside America's Pursuit of Its Enemies since 9/11* (New York: Simon & Schuster, 2007), 62 ("The Cheney Doctrine [after 9/11 became] 'Even if there's just a one percent chance of the unimaginable coming true, act as if it is a certainty.'").

[9] August 5, 2003, press briefing by U.S. Secretary of Defense Rumsfeld (addressing the discovery in Iraq of a Russian-built MiG-25R Foxbat B fighter aircraft).

gether, the result is that when there is even a scintilla of evidence of a looming threat, you must assume that it is a high probability; and that even if there is no evidence of even a 1 percent probability, that is not evidence of the absence of sufficient provocation to warrant attacking preemptively, and with overwhelming force. When such a collective mind-set prevails, evidence quickly gives way to hunches, intuitions, or gut instincts, with tragic consequences should those hunches prove unfounded.

Each of these three reasons is independently sufficient to rebut the claim that we should rely on *ex ante* legal standards to control unilateral preemptive attack. First, a legal defense does not constitute prior authorization. Second, humanitarian intervention is not preemptive intervention. And third, in practice, there are very few cases of pure multilateral prevention. When force is used, the rationale of prevention is often mixed in and disguised with other rationales. To add to the problem, there are very few cases of unilateral military action where there is adequate time to deliberate, so that law and legal argumentation can even enter the picture. This becomes very significant because, as a result, most of the cases that Doyle is discussing when he talks about preventive attack are actually cases involving mixed rationales, not pure cases of prevention.

The South Africa case he discusses is really a humanitarian intervention, which was multilateral, for the simple reason that sustained sanctions don't work unless they are multilateral. Similarly, the Cuban Missile Crisis should be remembered as a multilateral response that forestalled a unilateral preemptive strike by the U.S.

government upon missiles stationed in Cuba. The Missile Crisis was a situation in which, unlike the present day, there were lawyers of great ability participating, such as Abram Chayes, Nicholas Katzenbach, and Norbert Schlei.[10] The attorney general had extraordinary access directly to the president for the unique reason that he happened to be the president's brother. And famously, they had thirteen long days to deliberate.[11] What all this should tell us is that the Cuban Missile Crisis is as good as it gets when it comes to law's sinking into the decision-making process. In my experience, in these rooms, people do not tend to say, "I think the nation's survival is at stake. We must follow the law." Instead they tend to say, "Let the bastards sue us in the dark," or, as President Regan put it during the Iran Contra affair, "The American people will never forgive me if I fail to [act] over this legal question."[12]

Take the clearest recent example of this phenomenon: the 2003 Iraq war. Even after the UN Security Council passed Resolution 1441,[13] it was never clear whether a second Security Council resolution would be sought.[14] It remained unclear whether the rationale for attacking

[10] See generally Abram Chayes, *The Cuban Missile Crisis: International Crises and the Role of Law* (New York: Oxford University Press, 1974).

[11] See Robert F. Kennedy, *Thirteen Days: A Memoir of the Cuban Missile Crisis* (New York: W. W. Norton, 1969).

[12] Ann Wroe, *Lives, Lies and the Iran-Contra Affair* (London: I. B. Tauris, 1991), 195 (quoting President Reagan).

[13] S.C. Res. 1441, U.N. SCOR, 57th Sess., U.N. Doc. S/Res/1441 (2002).

[14] For fuller discussion of the legal rationale offered for the second

Iraq would be prevention, disarmament, regime change, humanitarian intervention, democracy promotion, or simply long-term peace and security. All of these rationales were floated at various points in the days leading up to the decision to attack, but once the attack occurred, the stated legal rationale actually offered by both the United States government and the British government for launching the attack never mentioned prevention. The U.S. legal case never formally asserted preemptive self-defense as a legal basis for the war, instead resting on the much narrower claim that Iraq was in material breach of UN Security Council Resolutions 678, 687, and 1441.[15] Similarly, the contested British

---

Gulf War, see Harold Hongju Koh, *On American Exceptionalism*, 55 Stanford L. Rev. 1479, 1515–26 (2003).

[15] Then-UN Ambassador John Negroponte's letter to the Security Council states, in relevant part:

> The actions being taken are authorized under existing Council resolutions, including resolution 678 (1990) and resolution 687 (1991). Resolution 687 imposed a series of obligations on Iraq, including, most importantly, extensive disarmament obligations, that were conditions of the cease-fire established under it. It has long been recognized and understood that a material breach of these obligations removes the basis of the cease-fire and revives the authority to use force under resolution 678. This has been the basis for coalition use of force in the past and has been accepted by the Council, as evidenced, for example, by the Secretary General's public announcement in January 1993 following Iraq's material breach of resolution 687 that coalition forces had received a mandate from the Council to use force according to resolution 678.
>
> Iraq continues to be in material breach of its disarmament obligations under resolution 687, as the Council affirmed in resolution 1441. Acting under the authority of Chapter VII of the UN Charter, the Council unani-

legal opinion justifying the war rested not on broad customary law arguments about preemptive self-defense,
but on two narrow arguments that Iraq had materially
breached a number of preexisting Security Council resolutions.[16] My point is that there are very few real-life
cases in which decision-makers genuinely rely on a pure,

---

mously decided that Iraq has been and remained in material breach of its
obligations and recalled its repeated warnings to Iraq that it will face serious consequences as a result of its continued violations of its obligations.
The resolution then provided Iraq a "final opportunity" to comply, but
stated specifically that violations by Iraq of its obligations under resolution
1441 to present a currently accurate, full and complete declaration of all
aspects of its weapons of mass destruction programs and to comply with
and cooperate fully in the resolution's implementation would constitute a
further material breach.

The government of Iraq decided not to avail itself of its final opportunity
under resolution 1441 and has clearly committed additional violations. In
view of Iraq's material breaches, the basis for the cease-fire has been removed, and use of force is authorized under resolution 678.

Iraq repeatedly has refused, over a protracted period of time, to respond
to diplomatic overtures, economic sanctions, and other peaceful means designed to help bring about Iraqi compliance with its obligations to disarm
and to permit full inspection of its WMD and related programs. The actions
that coalition forces are undertaking are an appropriate response. They are
necessary steps to defend the United States and the international community from the threat posed by Iraq and to restore international peace and
security in the area. Further delay would simply allow Iraq to continue its
unlawful and threatening conduct.

Letter from UN Ambassador John Negroponte to Ambassador Ma-
mady Traore, President of the Security Council (March 20, 2003),
available at http://www.usembassy.it/file2003_03/alia/A3032109.htm.

[16] Lord Goldsmith, the attorney general, placed the following par-
liamentary answer into the *Times* (London):

multilateral prevention rationale in a deliberative framework that allows law to enter the picture so that Doyle's
proposed legal standards might realistically be applied.

My fourth objection is that I don't think that Doyle's
standards will operate as he hopes with regard to unilateral interventions. The "Four *L*" standards are just too
easily manipulated by those who want to use military

Authority to use force against Iraq exists from the combined effect of resolutions 678, 687 and 1441. All of these resolutions were adopted under
Chapter VII of the UN Charter which allows the use of force for the express purpose of restoring international peace and security:

1. In resolution 678 the Security Council authorised force against Iraq,
   to eject it from Kuwait and to restore peace and security in the area.

2. In resolution 687, which set out the ceasefire conditions after Operation Desert Storm, the Security Council imposed continuing obligations on Iraq to eliminate its weapons of mass destruction in order to
   restore international peace and security in the area. Resolution 687
   suspended but did not terminate the authority to use force under resolution 678.

3. A material breach of resolution 687 revives the authority to use force
   under resolution 678.

4. In resolution 1441 the Security Council determined that Iraq has
   been and remains in material breach of resolution 687, because it has
   not fully complied with its obligations to disarm under that resolution.

5. The Security Council in resolution 1441 gave Iraq "a final opportunity to comply with its disarmament obligations" and warned Iraq of
   the "serious consequences" if it did not.

6. The Security Council also decided in resolution 1441 that, if Iraq
   failed at any time to comply with and cooperate fully in the implementation of resolution 1441, that would constitute a further material breach.

7. It is plain that Iraq has failed so to comply and therefore Iraq was at
   the time of resolution 1441 and continues to be in material breach.

force.[17] For an example, look at a recent *Yale Law Journal* article by Jide Nzelibe and John Yoo. That essay paints a "funhouse mirror" picture of the kind of deliberative process that Doyle is describing, applied by two lawyers who really believe in executive power.[18]

The fact of the matter is that legal standards rarely

---

8. Thus, the authority to use force under resolution 678 has revived and so continues today.

9. Resolution 1441 would in terms have provided that a further decision of the Security Council to sanction force was required if that had been intended. Thus, all that resolution 1441 requires is reporting to and discussion by the Security Council of Iraq's failures, but not an express further decision to authorise force.

I have lodged a copy of this answer, together with resolutions 678, 687 and 1441 in the Library of both Houses.

"Lord Goldsmith's Statement," *Times* (London), March 18, 2003, at A2. In response to that assertion, the deputy legal adviser to the foreign secretary, Elizabeth Wilmhurst, resigned from the Foreign Office. See Ewen MacAskill, "Adviser Quits Foreign Office over Legality of War," *Guardian*, March 23, 2003, at 1; see also letter to the editor, "War Would Be Illegal," *Guardian*, March 7, 2003, at 13 (letter signed by sixteen professors of international law at Oxford, Cambridge, London, and Paris asserting the illegality of a war convened without a second Security Council resolution).

[17] Doyle acknowledges that "we retain good reasons to keep the law as simple, as bright a line as possible, in order to discourage self-serving interpretation." Nevertheless, the four-part test he advocates hardly constitutes the kind of simple, bright-line test that might succeed in forestalling self-serving interpretations.

[18] Jide Nzelibe and John Yoo, *Rational War and Constitutional Design*, 115 Yale L.J. 2512 (2006). For a criticism of Nzelibe and Yoo's argument, see Harold Hongju Koh, *Setting the World Right*, 115 Yale L.J. 2350, 2374–78 (2006).

work in these circumstances to prevent an illegal use of force. You have to ban it and grant no exceptions. And then, if somebody wants to violate that ban, they should seek forgiveness, not prior permission. That means they should seek to be pardoned, not receive some kind of prior immunity before undertaking their acts. However reasonable Doyle's legal test may appear to be in the abstract, in practice, it is far too ornate and complicated. How, realistically, can individuals, much less bureaucracies, unilaterally apply this complex four-part test with all of its subparts? And if Doyle concedes that they are all balancing tests, do we have any doubt as to how those tests would balance out under real-life circumstances? If we want to create a meaningful default position against unwarranted use of force, in these emergency situations, we need bright-line rules. That is what *Miranda* warnings have taught us: the need for a prophylactic rule to protect the rights of individuals taken into police custody.[19] Government officials must understand exactly what they are or are not forbidden by law to do, and to understand equally that if they take illegal actions, they will surely be sued.

What are some of the dangers of a per se ban on unilateral preemptive force? First, phony multilateralism: to get access to these multilateral standards, you might find powerful nations creating "coalitions of the willing," as the United States did to support the second Gulf

---

[19] See Miranda v. Arizona, 384 U.S. 436 (1966) (requiring as a prophylactic rule that every criminal suspect in the United States be warned of his or her right to consult with an attorney and right against self-incrimination before being questioned by the police).

War. But here is the advantage of Step One of Doyle's approach: applying these standards multilaterally by working through established institutions and established multilateral institutions. If you make these decisions regarding the use of force through established organizations, rather than ad hoc coalitions of the willing, then you will find yourself in situations like the OAS Resolution in the Cuban Missile Crisis, where there was a formal mechanism for determining whether other allies truly agreed that regional force should be used. Or to take a counterexample, when the Organization of Eastern Caribbean States (OECS) voted a resolution approving the 1984 U.S. invasion of Grenada, it was possible to say that the OECS was primarily an organization to foster economic and financial unity among the eastern Caribbean states, not a mutual security pact or war-making organization, and thus that the resolution was *ultra vires*. In a standing institution, there is also an opportunity to table a resolution that terminates the use of force, as occurred in the UN as the Kosovo bombing wore on.

Similarly, I think it an error to apply these standards, as Doyle would do, to attacks against private parties, such as terrorists holding weapons of mass destruction. This strikes me as a mistaken mixing of apples with oranges. Terrorists are covered by antiterrorism law and criminal law; they should not be made part of a legal standard that enables regional multilateral action through multilateral organizations and coalitions of the willing against nation-states. To go down that path will lead to confusion and make Doyle's "Four *L*'s" even harder to apply.

The fifth and final concern with Doyle's approach is

the problem of knowledge, proof, and prediction. In a crisis, people tend to believe what they want to believe. The question of what you want to believe can turn very much on what kind of information you think is relevant. Doyle gives the example of Iraq, where in fact we have learned many things after the fact, in a postmortem autopsy, that we could not have predicted *ex ante.*

Applying Doyle's test, how would the four factors of lethality, likelihood, legality, and legitimacy now balance out for or against a preemptive strike against North Korea's Kim Jong-il? Having spent several days in the presence of Kim Jong-il when I went to North Korea with Secretary of State Madeleine Albright in the fall of 2000, I know that an observer could perceive him either as a rational actor or as a person who often is just plain unpredictable. If we cannot be sure which is which, how can we rationally make the predictions that Doyle's "Four *L*'s" test would like us to make? And how do we make sure that we accurately project and weigh the costs and benefits of a preemptive attack? After all, Donald Rumsfeld, former secretary of defense, projected *ex ante* that the cost of the Iraq war would be less than $50 billion, a far cry from the $2 trillion plus it has turned out to cost.[20] As Tom Ricks points out in his chilling book, *Fiasco,* "[T]he intellectual acrobatics [involved in] simultaneously 'worst-casing' the threat presented by Iraq while 'best-casing' the subsequent cost and difficulty of occupying the country" teaches that a

[20] Martin Wolk, "Cost of Iraq War Could Surpass $1 Trillion," MSNBC.COM, March 17, 2006, http://www.msnbc.msn.com/id/11880954.

truly rational weighing of costs and benefits, of the type that Doyle would favor, can only rarely be conducted before the fact.[21]

This is why I call for two cheers for Michael Doyle's standards for conducting anticipatory war. Make no mistake. We do need legal standards and they should be applied in multilateral situations, but I am firmly opposed to suggesting that individual nations should have the freedom to apply those standards to their own decisions to engage in unilateral preemption. Legal defenses cannot preauthorize. Nor is humanitarian intervention the correct analogy, because humanitarian intervention does not trigger humanitarian retaliation, because there are external constraints on multilateral intervention, and because there are so few pure cases of multilateral prevention.

A far better approach would be to maintain a unilateral ban on unilateral preemptive attacks. Those nations who feel compelled to ignore that ban could seek subsequent forgiveness and not prior permission, much as President Harry Truman did when he dropped the atomic bomb on the civilian population of Nagasaki. That is not the kind of drastic action that should be preauthorized. If the president feels compelled so to act, and he wants to argue that he was motivated to do so in the name of national survival, he can defend himself in many different legal and political fora. A prosecutor could decline to prosecute him, he could receive a pardon, or his sentence could be commuted. But we should

[21] Thomas E. Ricks, *Fiasco: The American Military Adventure in Iraq* (New York: Penguin Press, 2006), 4.

reject the notion that he should be given the freedom and authorization *ex ante* to undertake such drastic action.

If we go down the route that Doyle suggests, we are likely to see many more sham coalitions of the willing. We will witness many more situations in which unilateral preemptive military action is taken based on hunches, in the face of insuperable problems of knowledge, proof, and prediction. Down that road await cycles of retaliation. And that is why, in spite of my great admiration for Michael Doyle, I can accept only two of the three cornerstones of his argument.

COMMENT

RICHARD TUCK

For a line of political philosophers running from antiquity down to the eighteenth century, the question with which Michael Doyle has been dealing in these two brilliant essays was not merely an issue in the relationship between states: it was the only question there *is* in political theory itself. This conviction was particularly marked among sixteenth- and seventeenth-century writers, who had witnessed the incessant and unscrupulous wars of their age, from the vicious little campaigns of the Italian city-states through to the all-out conflict and devastation of the Thirty Years War, and who derived from this experience a keen sense of the fragile character of peace among any groups of human beings. The insights of these writers culminated in the theories of Hugo Grotius and Thomas Hobbes (Grotius, we should not forget, who was hailed later in the century as the founder of the modern science of morality, not as a theorist of international law).

Although Jefferson McMahan, and to some extent Professor Doyle, talk as if there was only one tradition of "just war" theory, in fact there are at least two equally powerful and influential traditions. One is the Augustinian or theological model, according to which military action by states should be governed by the same principles as judicial acts by governments over their citizens. But theorists in the Grotius-Hobbes tradition belonged to a rival tradition, defined by the idea that human life is governed by two minimalist moral principles. One is that that we are always entitled to defend ourselves against attack, including taking reasonable preventive steps where we judge a genuine danger exists; and the other is that we should never inflict unnecessary harm upon another human being. (For Hobbes, these two principles correspond in effect to his "right of nature" and "law of nature"). In this sense, and to some people's surprise today, Hobbes as much as Grotius presumed that there is no fundamental *moral* conflict, and that "all men" or, as he sometimes said, "all the world" would accept these two principles.[1]

It should be stressed that these writers were as unhappy as Professor Doyle is with the other, theological, strand of thinking about preventive war, which proclaimed that only *actual* attack could justify self-defensive action: for all the reasons that Professor Doyle gave in his first essay, they recognized that serious political theory had to accept that any justification for self-

[1] For a full discussion of this, see my *Rights of War and Peace* (New York: Oxford University Press, 1999).

defense has to include a justification for preventive action. As Cassius Dio reported Cicero as saying, in a phrase often quoted by Renaissance and seventeenth-century writers, "Do not wait until you have suffered some such [attack] and then rue it, but be on your guard before you suffer; for it is rash to allow dangers to come upon you and then to repent of it, when you might have anticipated them."[2]

For Grotius, this was the end of the matter. We could agree upon the moral principles that permitted judicious prevention, and we could also agree upon which actions were indeed requisite for our defense and which inflicted unnecessary damage upon our enemy. But for Hobbes, the difficulties would only just be beginning when we agreed on the principles: we will need political institutions precisely because we cannot agree on the question of what then *counts* as necessary. Conflict arises between men not because of disagreement over the basic framework for peaceful coexistence, but over what one might call the epistemic or factual question of whether we *actually* need to take action against a possible enemy, and only submission to a common authority with power to decide this factual question can stop constant preventive warfare.

An interesting example of this is actually to be found in the writing of someone whose lectures Hobbes may have attended, Alberico Gentili, the professor of civil law at Oxford University—a figure who is by no means

[2] Cassius Dio, *Roman History,* ed. Herbert Baldwin Foster, trans. Earnest Cary (Cambridge, MA: Loeb Classical Library, 1969), 4: 472–73 (45.35–366).

marginal, and indeed is generally regarded as one of the founders of modern international law. He was very influential on Grotius, but he was also in many ways an extreme adherent of the sort of theory I am discussing. Gentili held that the mere existence of a superpower—one that is enormously more powerful than its neighbors—is itself intrinsically a threat to the rest of the world. He was referring to Spain, which he thought by virtue of its American empire had grotesquely distorted the balance of power in Europe. The mere power of Spain, said Gentili, was sufficient grounds to treat it as a potential threat to other nations and to attack it pre-emptively.[3] And indeed, I think it is true to say that when the English attacked Spain under Queen Elizabeth, Francis Drake and the rest were in fact acting on Gentili's principles, since at that point Spain had not attacked them.[4] They took the view that the mere existence of an enormously powerful state was itself a threat requiring a military response.

We may disagree with the Elizabethans, but what they thought is a good example of the sort of reasoning that you might be led to once you start asking yourself questions such as, what is the evidence for a threat? What does its likelihood rest on? History may tell us that immensely powerful imperial powers act in certain dangerous ways. That will then be reasonable evidence, though

[3] See Alberico Gentili, *De Iure Belli*, ed. C. Phillipson, trans. J. C. Rolfe (Oxford: Clarendon, 1933), 2:62–65. The first edition was in 1588.

[4] For this, see, e.g., Geoffrey Parker, *The Grand Strategy of Philip II* (New Haven: Yale University Press, 1998), 170 ff.

not conclusive evidence, that the imperial powers of our day may do the same. So these are very dangerous and difficult waters in which to sail.

What Professor Doyle in effect has done is to throw down a gauntlet to Hobbes or Gentili on behalf of Grotius: it is possible, he says, for us to have broadly convincing methods of deciding whether a course of action is indeed necessary or not, and even though there may be no institution with the power to determine the question for us, we are not faced with the prospect of reasonable agents finding themselves incapable of peaceful coexistence. What might a Hobbesian skeptic say in reply?

He would certainly have little to quarrel about as far as Professor Doyle's first three conditions go. *Lethality* and *likelihood* together cover the requirement that the self-defensive action is necessary—that is, that the threat is both grave and likely. *Legitimacy* is Professor Doyle's term for the second of the two fundamental principles I just mentioned, since it requires us to limit our action to the minimum required to avoid unnecessary or disproportionate harm to our adversary, or to other people caught up in the conflict. As Hobbes said, "there are some natural laws whose observance does not cease even in war. For I can not see what ... cruelty (which is vengeance without regard to future good) contribute[s] to any man's peace or preservation." Disproportionate or unnecessary harm is precisely what Hobbes termed "cruelty." Incidentally, when Professor Doyle says in his essay that "proportionality should be more strictly required in preventive actions" than in response to an actual armed attack, I think he's actually going somewhat further than these seventeenth-century writers would have done. By and large they took the same requirement of proportionality strictly to apply both to preventive measures and to actual defense. That is to say, when you're engaged in an actual war, the ban on cruelty still applies: you should not treat the soldiers of your enemy in a cruel or unnecessarily violent fashion.

The skeptic would be rather more puzzled about the last condition, *legality*. Professor Doyle's idea here seems to be that there is an existing body of international jurisprudence, the force of which in some sense states acknowledge, but there is no institution whose determination on the matter *eo ipso* decides the question (since the whole point of Professor Doyle's discussion I take to be that the UN Security Council is not necessarily a reliable or authoritative institution of this kind). Our judgment about legality is then the same kind of thing as our judgment about necessity or proportionality: we *ourselves* have to assess whether the proposed action fits the accepted canons of international law. But those canons are themselves subject to dispute and require interpretation; moreover, one of the few things about which there is little disagreement, as both Grotius and Hobbes observed, is precisely that a proportionate response to a real danger is a legitimate course of action for a state, or an individual. If the first three conditions are genuinely met, that would therefore seem to settle the question of *legality*. The one exception is that (on Professor Doyle's argument) a state must at least put the question to the Security Council first before taking action. The skeptic might say that this is rather like the fetial law of the Romans: a ceremonious rather than a substantive requirement for the initiation of war.

Doyle also hints that retrospective judgment by the Security Council might validate or invalidate preventive military actions. This heads in the direction of the sort of idea that Dean Koh suggests in his comments, namely, that we keep in place a "bright-line" prohibition on preventive war but allow that particular circumstances might provide a defense based on necessity. But in his first essay Doyle seems to rule out this sort of proposal. The thrust of his argument is that we must leave a space for unilateral action by states, or multilateral action without Security Council sanction: action that is not and may never be sanctioned by the Security Council. Therefore retrospective judgment, though useful and possibly informative, cannot be critical in the way that the skeptic might expect.

So the skeptic would find in the end little to dissent from as far as the four conditions go. But equally, he would find little to force him out of his skepticism. After all, Hobbes, as I said, entirely accepted the Grotian *moral* framework: it was the further step of actually implementing it without an authoritative decision-making body at which he balked. And indeed, as I said earlier, that is the fundamental issue in politics: that is why you create a state, precisely in order to have an institution of the sort that can and will settle disagreements about when and how the generally agreed principles will be applied.

So where does this leave us if we join Professor Doyle

in accepting the principle of preventive war? How do we respond institutionally and procedurally, given the absence of a transnational sovereign? I detect two different responses to this question in the essays. Sometimes Doyle suggests that there will be public discussion not just about the principles themselves—there is unlikely to be much discussion about the principles, since on the whole I think most people would agree to them fairly rapidly—but about the application of the principles in particular circumstances. And if we have a discussion, Doyle suggests, this will shame states or the Security Council itself into acting in accordance with what has emerged from the discussion. On this model, which is not unfamiliar, there is a sort of global public authority of a rather diffuse kind, which might control particular states, and even the Security Council itself. Hobbes would be slightly puzzled by this. He might doubt that this forum for discussion, out of which comes a decision, is going to have a binding or limiting force on the people who took part in the discussion. Can one imagine the result of such a discussion as having anything like the force of the decrees of a statelike institution or sovereign body?

There is a different model that sometimes appears in what Doyle has said, which is that the Security Council itself retains authority, but that it should act according to a set of new internal rules that should govern its deliberations. Obviously the two models may overlap in various ways; they are sharply separable in ideal terms, but they might be combined in practice. Either way, though, Doyle does seem to envisage some kind of institutional implementation of his principles. This is an enormously important question—as I said, for Hobbes, it is the most important question there could be in political theory. The creation of a new institutional form with real authority to decide would be in effect the creation of a world sovereign. These are high stakes; so one would like to know more from Michael about the character of the institution or mechanism that he proposes. For example, if it is to be something like the Security Council, is it controllable by anything like democratic principles?

I will close by interjecting a plea for politics. Professor Doyle is critical of the way that political considerations often sway the UN and the Security Council. But when we are talking about such important decisions of war and peace, then, personally, I would rather have politics than impartial judicial decisions, just as I would rather have politics in the U.S. Congress or the British Parliament, as opposed to the determination of remote tribunals. If what we are talking about are the core functions of the state, politics is how we deal with these sorts of decisions. Ideally it will be democratic politics, even given that democratic politics can have all sorts of corrupt or unsatisfactory features. People make bargains for all sorts of reasons. But in the end, that is what we are used to as a way of handling our political life, and democratic politics—warts and all—achieves impressive levels of legitimacy.

But the skeptic, having said all this, would also say that no one has put these questions to a modern audience as clearly as Professor Doyle has done. Hobbes himself said, "to accuse, requires lesse Eloquence (such is mans Nature) than to excuse,"[5] and having read and listened to Professor Doyle, I am consumed with admiration for his intellectual elegance, and disinclined to disagree too far with such a persuasive scholar.

[5] *Leviathan* Chapter XIX, p. 97 original edition (Cambridge ed. p. 132).

COMMENT

Jeff McMahan

🮱

I find myself in the awkward position—awkward, that is, for a commentator—of agreeing with virtually all aspects of Michael Doyle's powerful critique of what international law and current U.S. doctrine imply about preventive war, and with most of his constructive suggestions for a new set of laws, institutions, and policies for addressing threats to national and international security that seem both real and serious but are not imminent. Yet, although what he says is largely right, there is more to be said. There is an important moral constraint on preventive war that he largely overlooks (though it is faintly indicated in his early reference to a "responsible party" condition for justified self-defense), and that fails to appear in his list of criteria for justified preventive action. I propose to devote these brief remarks to supplying the condition that is omitted from his account but that needs to be included.

My argument is intended as a friendly refinement of Doyle's account, and I have reason to hope that he will see it as such and regard it with favor. For he is well known for having certain allegiances to a Kantian approach to international relations, and the condition that I believe is missing from his account should be of particular concern to Kantians.

Perhaps the best way to introduce the objection to preventive war on which I will focus is to note how the aim of averting future threats has been treated in the traditional theory of the just war. Although theorists of the just war have articulated various positions on the permissibility of preventive war, there is one view that is particularly well represented within the tradition. In the theory of the just war, the requirement that there be a just cause for war is a component of the doctrine of *jus ad bellum*—that is, the set of principles governing the *resort* to war. The idea that war must have a just cause has typically been understood as a restriction on the types of goal—or the types of good—that can justify the resort to war. But the application of the requirement cannot be restricted just to the resort to war. If a war in progress *continues* in the absence of a just cause—if, for example, its just cause has been achieved but it goes on nonetheless—it ceases to be just, and usually ceases to be permissible. The requirement of just cause therefore applies not only to the resort to war but also to the continuation of war. It is continuously applicable throughout the course of a war. It is, in other words, not only a condition of the legitimate resort to war but a general restriction on the types of goal that can *permissibly be pursued by means of war.*

This understanding of the requirement of just cause opens up the possibility that there can be just causes for war that cannot on their own justify the resort to war, even when all the other necessary conditions of a just war are satisfied. Perhaps there are goals that may permissibly be pursued by means of war, but only in conjunction with the pursuit of some other just goal or goals that can justify the initial resort to war. This is the way that the goal of averting future threats, or preventing future wrongs, has often been conceived within the just war tradition. Various theorists have held that while it is not permissible to go to war solely to avert some future threat, preventive action may nevertheless become permissible once an adversary is guilty of a wrong that independently justifies going to war. If, for example, an adversary is engaged in aggression, making it permissible to go to war in self-defense, it may *then* be permissible to use *additional* force in the course of the defensive action, or even *after* the goal of self-defense has been achieved, in order to disarm the adversary, thereby preventing further threats from arising in the future. According to this view, military action to disarm the adversary that would not have been permissible in the absence of aggression becomes permissible once aggression has occurred.

Grotius, for example, writes that "it is permissible to forestall an act of violence which is not immediate but which is seen to be threatening from a distance; not directly—for that, as we have shown, would work injustice—but indirectly, by inflicting punishment for a crime commenced but not yet carried through."[1] By "directly" Grotius means action that has as its sole purpose and sole justification the forestalling of an uncertain future threat. He follows Augustine, Aquinas, and others in holding that punishment of wrongdoing is a just cause for war, and also holds that prevention and deterrence of future wrongdoing are among the legitimate functions of punishment. This passage may therefore be interpreted as asserting that once an adversary has begun a criminal war, it can then be permissible in the course of the war to use force to eliminate more distant threats from this same adversary.

The view that I am attributing to Grotius was appealing to classical just war theorists at least in part because they tended to conceive of war as punishment for wrongdoing. If war is a form of punishment, it should not be surprising that many of the classical theorists object to war that is purely preventive, for—at least until the arrival of the Bush administration—civilized peoples

---

[1] Hugo Grotius, *De Jure Belli ac Pacis Libris Tres,* trans. Francis W. Kelsey (Oxford: Clarendon Press, 1925; reprint, Buffalo, NY: William S. Hein & Co., 1995), bk. 2, chap. 1, sec. 16, p. 184. The passage to which he refers in which he rejects "direct" preventive punishment is bk. 2, chap. 1, sec. 5, pp. 173–75. Vitoria advances a view quite similar to Grotius's. For unusually perceptive commentary on the views of Grotius, Vitoria, Gentili, and Vattel on preventive war, see Gregory M. Reichberg, "Preventive War in Classical Just War Theory," *Journal of the History of International Law* 9 (2007): 5–33.

have tended to reject the permissibility of preventive punishment, including preventive detention.

There are at least two good reasons why preventive punishment is objectionable. One is that the evidence for a person's being dangerous is generally insufficient to justify harming him until he demonstrates his dangerousness by actually committing a crime. But while this consideration supports the rejection of preventive punishment *in law,* it does not show that purely preventive punishment would always, as Grotius says, "work injustice." For there are other forms of evidence that in many cases are better predictors of future criminal action than the actual commission of a single crime. Preventive action taken on the basis of such evidence might be less likely to be unnecessary, and therefore less likely to be unjust, than preventive action taken in response to a single criminal act.

The second reason why preventive punishment is objectionable reinforces the first but is deeper and less contingent. It is that it is only when a person has actually *done* something wrong that he has made himself morally *liable* to be harmed as a means of fulfilling the goals of punishment, including the prevention of future wrongdoing. Punishment is unjust in the absence of a crime. It is this consideration that I think best explains the view of preventive defense found in the writings of Grotius and other classical just war theorists. When a country has not yet acted in a way that makes it responsible for an unjust threat to another, it (or, more precisely, its individual agents) cannot be liable to defensive action. Yet if the country is already guilty of wrongful action, such as initiating an unjust war, and stopping the action or rectifying its consequences constitutes a just cause for war, then it can be permissible, in the course of pursuing that just cause, to take further action to preempt the possibility of further wrongful action in the future. The wrongful action that exposes the aggressor to defensive action now also makes it liable to further, preventive action as well.[2]

Most of us, of course, do not regard war as a form of punishment. The principal—and to many people the only—just cause for war is defense against aggression. But defense is subject to the same condition that governs punishment—namely, that a person must engage in certain forms of action in order to become morally liable to harmful defensive action. A person who has done nothing to lose or compromise his right not to be attacked remains innocent in the relevant sense. To attack him would be unjust.

That a person is likely to act in a certain way in the future cannot, it seems, make him morally liable to attack now. To harm him preventively before he acts is to fail to respect his capacity for autonomy, which enables him, even if he has decided to act wrongly, to continue to deliberate and to alter his decision. Of course, people

---

[2] For a contemporary defense of a view of this sort, see Jeff McMahan and Robert McKim, "The Just War and the Gulf War," *Canadian Journal of Philosophy* 23, no. 4 (1993): 501–41. I have subsequently come to have doubts about this view. For an able defense of the view against my later criticisms, see Thomas Hurka, "Liability and Just Cause," *Ethics and International Affairs* 21, no. 2 (2007): 199–218.

generally have the capacity to change their mind right up to the time of decisive action, but effective defensive action cannot wait till then. So potential wrongdoers cannot be allowed every possible opportunity to draw back from wrongdoing. In the law, certain forms of action that are preliminary to the commission of certain crimes—forms of action such as planning and preparation—have themselves been made criminal. They are, in other words, treated as sufficient for liability to criminal sanction. The idea is, roughly, that those who have engaged in planning and preparing for the commission of a certain crime have done enough to raise the risk of criminal action to make themselves liable to action necessary to prevent the crime. That they have acted in these ways denies them a justified complaint if they are forcibly prevented from completing the crime.

A parallel form of justification might be invoked to justify preventive war. Suppose, for example, that our intelligence services have compelling, indeed decisive, evidence that the political leaders of another country are planning and preparing for an aggressive war against us a year from now. Suppose that diplomacy and other nonmilitary options would be unavailing, and that if we wait until the attack is imminent, or even until it actually occurs, our chances of successful defense will be significantly lower and our expected casualties significantly higher. As in the case of a domestic conspiracy, the leaders of this country have engaged in culpable action that seems sufficient to make them liable to preventive measures.

Suppose, however, that so far *only* the political leaders have been involved in the planning. Military personnel, and in particular the rank-and-file soldiers, do not yet know anything about the unjust war being planned. They are at their bases, doing the things that soldiers do in peacetime: training, drilling, and so on. Unlike the political leaders, they have so far done nothing culpable, nor even anything to raise the risks we face from their country. So it seems questionable whether they have done anything to make themselves individually liable to preventive attack.

I will call this the example of the "Unmobilized Military." It may not pose a problem if we adopt a collectivist approach to war, according to which, as Rousseau says, war is something that takes place not among individual people but between states. On this kind of view, the action of the leaders makes the *state itself* liable, including its soldiers. I think, however, that this sort of collectivist view is untenable. One reason why this is so is that it makes mere membership in the state a ground of liability, even when membership is involuntary, thereby making liability to preventive defense independent of action or choice. Another is that it seems to support a doctrine of total war, since combatants and noncombatants are equally members of the state and therefore should all be liable if the state itself is liable.

Yet if we insist that individuals cannot be legitimate targets of attack in war unless they have acted in a way that makes them personally liable to attack, it becomes difficult to see how preventive war could be just in cases of this sort, when many or most of those who would have to be attacked may have joined the military for good reasons and are entirely unaware that their political leaders are plotting aggression. It seems that these unmobilized soldiers are innocent in the relevant sense.

This is a particularly clear implication of the currently orthodox theory of the just war. It is usually assumed that this theory objects to preventive war on two strong though defeasible grounds. The objections derive from two principles of *jus ad bellum*. One is the principle of last resort. Since the threat that preventive war would address is by definition not imminent, there is time to try options other than war; hence war cannot be the last resort. This is a familiar objection, but I think it is misplaced. It is a mistake to interpret the relevant requirement as requiring that war can be justified only when no other option remains to be tried. It is better to understand the requirement as a requirement of necessity. If a temporally remote threat can be averted now but not later when it becomes imminent, preventive war may satisfy a requirement of necessity.

The other *jus ad bellum* principle that is often thought to count against preventive war is proportionality. Assuming that the temporal remoteness of a threat is correlated with a lower probability of its eventuating, future threats have to be discounted for reduced probability, and this tends to make preventive war disproportionate.

But what has been little noticed, though it ought to be even more obvious, is that preventive war is decisively ruled out by the orthodox understanding of the just war theory's requirement of discrimination. In its most generic formulation, the requirement of discrimination is simply the requirement to direct intentional attacks only against legitimate targets. According to the currently dominant version of the theory of the just war, only combatants are legitimate targets. Noncombatants are not. The rationale for claiming that the distinction between combatants and noncombatants coincides with the distinction between legitimate and illegitimate targets is that only combatants pose a threat; only they may be attacked defensively. Noncombatants are mere bystanders and are therefore morally immune to attack. (In the contemporary literature, the requirement of discrimination is often referred to as the "principle of noncombatant immunity.") Only those who are engaged in the activity of war have combatant status, for only they are actively threatening. While unmobilized soldiers in peacetime may wear a uniform and even carry a gun, they are not actively threatening anyone and thus are not combatants in the sense in which that term is understood in the theory of the just war. (Whether they have combatant status under international law is a different issue.) But because unmobilized soldiers in peacetime are not combatants, in that they are not engaged in the activity of war, and because preventive war is *defined* as war against those who are not currently engaged in war, nor poised for imminent engagement in war, it follows that on the currently dominant theory of the just war, unmobilized soldiers cannot be legitimate targets of attack. According to this theory, there are no legitimate targets in preventive war. Preventive war is necessarily indiscriminate and therefore cannot be permissibly fought.

That the orthodox theory has this implication may not show that preventive war cannot be permissible. It might instead show, as I believe, that the orthodox theory is mistaken. In my view, the orthodox theory is mistaken in holding that posing a threat to others is the criterion of liability to attack in war. Although I will not argue for this claim here, I believe that the criterion of liability to attack in war is moral responsibility for a wrong, or a threatened wrong—such as a threat of wrongful harm—that it is permissible to prevent or rectify by means of war.

According to this criterion, the political leaders in the case of the Unmobilized Military who are planning and preparing for an aggressive war may be morally liable to attack, for they have acted in a way that makes them responsible for a threat of unjust war. But suppose that it is not possible to attack them. Or suppose that there is a secret shadow government, whose members' identities are unknown, that knows about the plans for war and that will come to power if the existing leaders are killed. The members of this second-string government have been persuaded, as have the members of the general population, that we harbor aggressive designs against their country. Hence if we were to attempt to avert the threat of future attack by assassinating the existing leadership, this would appear to confirm the claims they had made to their successors. We would appear to be the aggressors and would be attacked in apparent self-defense. In these circumstances, we could not prevent an attack against us by preventive assassination only. Preventive war against the military would be necessary.

But, again, the members of the military have no knowledge of the aggressive plans of the political leaders and, we may suppose, have no reason even to suspect that such plans might be formulated. It does not seem that they can be held in any way responsible for the threat their leaders pose.

Most people do not accept that moral responsibility for an unjust threat is a necessary condition of liability to defensive force. Many will say that it does not matter that the unmobilized soldiers bear no responsibility for the threat, and that it does not even matter that they are not currently posing a threat. For them to be permissible targets it is sufficient that they are combatants—that is, that they wear the uniform and are armed, even if they are on their home base. But suppose that an American soldier goes now to a Swedish army base and kills a soldier there. The moral objection to this is not merely that the American soldier is acting without orders. This is an act of murder. The Swedish soldier is not a combatant in any morally relevant sense, and he has done nothing to lose his right not to be attacked, even by a member of a foreign military. Merely being an active-duty member of a military organization is not sufficient to make a person a legitimate target of attack.

The natural thought at this point is to suppose that in the case of the Unmobilized Military, the soldiers whose leaders are plotting unjust aggression are liable to attack because they *will* unjustly attack us unless we take action now to stop them. But this criterion of liability to attack is too permissive. Suppose we are in a protracted war of attrition with an aggressor state in which there is universal conscription. This war is certain to continue for at least several more years. It is therefore true of the

140

boys and girls in their last years of high school that they will attack us within a few years. But that does not seem to make them liable to attack now. How, then, do they differ from the unsuspecting soldiers on their bases in the example of the Unmobilized Military?

The answer to this challenge—if there *is* a satisfactory answer—must be that the unmobilized soldiers in this example satisfy two conditions that are jointly sufficient for liability to attack. One is that they made a choice to enlist in the military, or to allow themselves to be conscripted into the military. They have thus *committed* themselves—or have at least given others good reason to believe they have—to fight if ordered to do so. The other is that they have had the bad luck to have political leaders who are preparing to order them to fight in an unjust war, thereby converting them into agents of injustice. The first of these conditions distinguishes the unmobilized soldiers from the high school children in our other hypothetical example. And the second condition distinguishes them from unmobilized soldiers whose leaders are not plotting unjust aggression.

It may seem that this suggestion revises my earlier claim that the criterion of liability to attack is moral responsibility for a wrong, or for a threatened wrong. For the unmobilized soldiers are entirely unaware of the threat their leaders pose. But in fact what this shows is that one can be responsible for a threat of which one is unaware. Because they have committed their wills to obedience, their wills have become extensions of the wills of the political leaders; thus they share in responsibility with the leaders for the threat of attack their country poses. They are the ones who will implement the attack, and their wills are conditionally committed to it, although they are not yet aware of this.

This proposal makes the liability of these soldiers *strict*, in the sense that they have become liable entirely without wrongdoing or fault. Imagine that the soldiers in Unmobilized Military are citizens of a country with no recent history of aggression, and that they joined in the reasonable expectation that they would not be ordered to fight in an unjust, aggressive war. Imagine as well that there is a neighboring country that has recently engaged in various unjust acts of aggression. Soldiers in this neighboring country who recently joined their country's military may have had good reason to expect that they would be commanded to fight in an unjust war. But in fact their leaders have decided not to engage in further aggression. According to the two conditions of liability I have proposed, these latter soldiers are not liable to attack, whereas the soldiers in Unmobilized Military are, despite the fact that they may have joined for admirable moral reasons. The soldiers in Unmobilized Military are simply the victims of bad moral luck. Their liability rests on their having chosen to join the military, or having chosen not to resist being inducted into it, together with their having had the bad luck of serving a government that is plotting aggression.

It is important to notice that my claim is that the unmobilized soldiers are strictly liable based on their prior choice to enter the military, knowing what military organizations do. I do not claim that they are liable to attack merely by virtue of being part of a collective, in this

142

case the military. If membership in the military were genuinely involuntary, as membership in an ethnic or national group is, it could not be a basis of liability. Liability is not a matter of identity but of choice and action.

I suspect that many people will find this proposed solution to the problem of liability plausible. In that case one may wonder why I have belabored the problem when the solution is so simple. One reason is that the solution is neither as complete nor as satisfactory as one would like.

The solution is incomplete because some unmobilized soldiers whose government is plotting aggression may not be liable even by reference to the two-part criterion I have proposed. Of some it may not be true that they have chosen to be in the military, while of others it may not be true that they will later pose an unjust threat.

In some cases people are dragooned into the military literally, or almost literally, at gunpoint. While even this extreme form of coercion leaves room for choice, it does not seem to be the sort of choice that can be the basis of strict liability.

In other cases, even some of those who have freely chosen to join the military will not later pose a threat. Some, for example, may have made a doubly conditional commitment to fight when they joined. They may have committed their wills to fight if ordered to do so but only if they will also believe that what they are being ordered to do is morally permissible. In most cases, of course, they could not announce the second of these conditions at the time of enlistment, but some people (though obviously not many) do serve in the military with a private reservation of this sort. If a currently unmobilized soldier would refuse to fight if ordered to engage in unjust aggression, it is not true of him now that he will later pose an unjust threat, even if his government is planning an unjust war; therefore he fails to meet the second condition of the criterion of liability that I have proposed.

Note also that there is a continuous turnover of personnel in the military. There is continuous recruitment and enlistment, paralleled by a continuous process of retirement. In the example of the Unmobilized Military, in which the political leaders' plan is to initiate an unjust war in a year's time, many of the soldiers who are on active duty now would have rotated out of the military before the unjust attack would occur. It is therefore not true of them that they will engage in an unjust attack in the future. They, too, fail to meet the second condition of the suggested criterion of liability for unmobilized soldiers.

Of course, in the case of those unmobilized soldiers who are not liable to attack for one of these reasons—that they did not choose to join, that they would refuse to fight in an unjust war, or that they would no longer be in the military when the aggression would occur—there is usually nothing publicly accessible that distinguishes them from others who are liable. For this and various other reasons, a preventive attack cannot discriminate between those unmobilized soldiers who are liable and those who are not. While it may be a reasonable presumption to make of *each* unmobilized soldier that his presence in the military is the result of choice and that he will fight when ordered to do so, one can be confident in virtually all cases that there are *some* soldiers of whom the presumption is false. One can be confident, in other words, that preventive war involves deliberately attacking and killing people of whom one knows that some are fully innocent in any relevant sense, though one cannot know which ones they are. It remains true, however, that those who are not liable to attack because they will refuse to fight in an unjust war or because no aggression will occur until after they have retired are nevertheless responsible for making it reasonable for their adversaries to believe that they will fight. Even though they are not liable to attack, it is not obvious that they would have a justified complaint against their adversaries if they were attacked.

This explains why I think that the proposed solution to the problem of liability is incomplete: it is almost inevitable that some of those who would be intentionally attacked in a preventive war would not be morally liable to attack. The reason why I think the proposed solution is less than fully satisfactory stems from the fact, noted earlier, that responsibility and therefore liability are matters of degree. Responsibility, moreover, is not a wholly causal notion. The degree of an agent's responsibility for an unjust threat is a function of subjective as well as objective factors: for example, his beliefs, motives, intentions, and so on. This means, I believe, that unmobilized soldiers may be liable to attack to varying degrees.

Consider two variants of the case of the Unmobilized Military. In the original version, the soldiers are citizens of a country with no record of recent aggression. Let us assume, further, that their government has been democratically elected, and that there has been no reason, either now or at the time the soldiers joined the military, to suspect that this government would even consider engaging in unjust aggression. In a second version of the case, the soldiers are citizens of a country whose present government is a dictatorship that has recently been guilty of various acts of unjust aggression and shows no evidence of reform. In this version, the soldiers could reasonably expect when they joined that they would be ordered to fight in an unjust war. In both versions of the example, the political leaders are plotting unjust aggression and the soldiers have no knowledge of this. I claim that the soldiers in the second version are responsible to a greater degree for the threat their country poses than the soldiers in the first, and that their liability to attack is therefore correspondingly greater.

What this means in practical terms is that the conditions that must be met for preventive war to be justified are more stringent in the first case than in the second, other things being equal. The difference in liability manifests itself most saliently in the application of the proportionality requirement. A war that would be just barely proportionate in the second case would not be proportionate in the first. For example, a threat that would be just barely grave enough to justify a preventive attack on the unmobilized soldiers in the second version would not be sufficiently grave to justify preventively attacking the soldiers in the first version, who may have joined the military for thoroughly admirable reasons. Or when the differences in cost and probability of success between going to war preventively and waiting until the threat became imminent would be just barely large enough to make preventive war proportionate in the second case, they would be insufficiently large to make it proportionate in the first.

These examples are, of course, highly artificial and minimally described. It is much less obvious how considerations of liability would affect the proportionality of preventive war in actual cases, in all their unruly complexity. Yet these considerations are both real and important, and must be taken into account in cases in which there is knowledge that is relevant to determining the degree to which those who would be attacked preventively are liable to such attack.

It is worth noting that in the actual cases that Doyle discusses—the sanctions against South Africa, the blockade of Cuba, and the strike against the Iraqi reactor—there were no intentional military attacks against people who could not plausibly be regarded as liable to attack. But this is true mainly because none of these was actually an instance of preventive war. Only in the case of Osirak was there an actual military attack, and that attack was intended to destroy only a facility. It was timed, as Doyle points out, to avoid human casualties to the greatest extent possible.

But genuine preventive wars generally have to include human beings among their intended targets. When that is the case, it is a condition of justification that those who are attacked should have done something to make themselves liable to attack. I therefore think that Doyle needs to include a fifth entry in his list of standards for preventive war. Fortunately, *liability* begins with an "*l*."

147

Response to Commentators

⌘

MICHAEL W. DOYLE

Having drawn on Professor Tuck's, Professor Mc-Mahan's, and Dean Koh's comments to improve the written version, I do not need to make extensive final comments except to identify what I see as the differences that remain. I see them as small, but one or two may be significant. I see three key differences.

The first difference, in today's world of nation-states, is that the anarchic condition of world politics cannot be corrected by world government. And, short of world government, given the lack of genuine global community, the best we can do is to establish norms that mitigate anarchy. This is the issue that informs Professor Tuck's comments. His comments in November and written remarks included here correctly point out that I am indeed relying on the efficacy of standards and norms, and that, inevitably, in a world lacking an authoritative and enforceable set of global institutions, these norms will not on their own provide a fully reliable order. In these respects, I rely more on Grotian international law than a Hobbesian (such as Richard Tuck) would find advisable. I accept that it will be far from a reliable world order, but that developing norms to govern anarchy is a worthwhile effort, rather than a harmful or counterproductive indulgence, even if it is incomplete.

One problem that Hobbes identified as central to cooperation under anarchy is epistemic, as Tuck argues here and much more fully elsewhere.[1] For Hobbes, only a Leviathan can reliably fix meanings and reduce conflict. Acknowledging the lack of such a global Leviathan, these lectures make a plea for the value of communication, reaching across the disputes, to identify norms that are both livable in a dangerous world and reflective of the more basic values of human rights and self-determination that are widely shared in the emerging international community. For states seeking to avoid conflict or having no deep reasons for conflict, these norms can be coordinating devices. Avoiding the triggering of justifiable prevention by making threats to the survival of other states, not mobilizing the military resources that give those threats credence: in a dangerous world these are signals of what it takes to secure a safe harbor from strife. In my view this is the best we can now do in the world as it is. These standards can be only preliminary and incomplete, and they lack the Hobbesian fixity to end all conflict. They are also designed to reflect deep moral duties and to begin to create the conditions of respect and trust preliminary to a more reliable international order (I refer here to Immanuel Kant's "Preliminary Articles" to *Perpetual Peace*).[2] Moreover, we cannot consistently adopt a Hobbesian approach, despite its logical attraction, nor do I see Richard Tuck as advocating this. To do so would neglect the commitments to global human dignity that are one of the few great ac-

---

[1] See his *Rights of War and Peace,* especially chap. 4.

[2] Immanuel Kant, *Kant's Political Writings,* ed. Hans Reiss (Cambridge: Cambridge University Press, 1970), 93–97.

complishments of the twentieth century (even if they were so often violated in practice).

The second difference concerns who is liable to attack. I see the same principles applying to both preventive and immediate wars of self-defense. I agree with Professor Jeff McMahan that those who are sanctioned should be indeed only those "liable," and those not liable should not be sanctioned. Preventive self-defense that includes both armed attack and coercive economic sanctions should respect the rules of war, avoiding noncombatants, respecting necessity, and hewing to proportionality. Soldiers are normally legitimate targets of war in a war of self-defense, once an armed attack has occurred, even if the soldiers are "innocent" in the sense of having been drafted or being poorly informed about the aims of the war. They retain rights in war—to surrender and decent treatment as prisoners of war. Provided they have individually abided by the laws of war, they face no prosecution. They are not liable for the crime of aggressive war for which their leaders may be liable. Preventive wars should not differ in this respect. If ordinary soldiers have done nothing, and it is their leaders who are planning and threatening aggressive war without their knowledge, it is the leaders alone who should be liable. And it is those leaders my principles of "legitimacy"—necessity and proportionality—will target. But if the war aims of the leaders are known, soldiers who enlist voluntarily become liable to being attacked, as soldiers are in war. At Osirak, the Israelis placed some Iraqi soldiers at risk, but clearly the attack was directed at those who were, in Jeff McMahan's sense, mobi-

lized—those scientists and engineers at the nuclear facilities. The attack on the al Qaeda training camp in Afghanistan also seems to have met these criteria. So did
the Cuban blockade, which put first at risk the Soviet
sailors shipping missiles to Cuba. Attacks that are
planned by leaders but do not mobilize soldiers are the
ones that can most likely be addressed by targeted responses, usually sanctions, on the leaders and planners—as the UN economic sanctions against Iran (so
far) are properly designed to do.

The third set of differences with Dean Harold Koh
look large, partly, I think, because he is such a zealous
advocate. But we agree on many points. First, we agree
that unilateral anticipatory self-defense should not be
judged preauthorized or legal unless it meets the bright-
line *Caroline* standards. Preemptive self-defense, to be
preauthorized, should be clearly justifiable as proportional and "overwhelming" in its necessity and respon-
sive to so "imminent" a threat as to leave "no choice of
means" and "no moment for deliberation." These cases
will be rare, fortunately. The Tokyo Military Tribunal
found what may have been one twentieth-century case
in the Netherlands declaration of war against Japan in
December 1941 after the Dutch authorities learned that
attacks on the Netherlands East Indies were planned in
conjunction with the December 7–8 attacks on the
Philippines.

Second, I think we agree that *all* other requests for authorization to coerce should always go to the Security
Council. Only the Security Council can legally preauthorize preventive self-defense. (Article 39 of the UN

Charter says that the Security Council can and "shall" determine threats to the peace and "shall decide" what to do about them.) We agree that the Security Council should be called upon to fulfill its responsibilities. This proposition is more radical than it seems. Many suggest that the Security Council should not be embarrassed when a veto is likely, because vetoes undermine Charter-based rule of law. In this way, some applauded the decision by the United States, the United Kingdom, and NATO allies to circumvent the Security Council when they took military action against Serbia in defense of the beleaguered Kosovars in 1999. My argument is that all nondefensive or nonpreemptive uses of force, whether humanitarian or preventive, should go to the Security Council in order for it to begin to assume the responsibility the Charter mandates for it to "decide" on what constitutes a legitimate use of force and what does not. Otherwise we will not build up, through case law, the set of standards that promote the rule of law by defining in more reliable and operational terms the standards of likelihood, lethality, legitimacy, and legality (the Four L's) that justify the preventive use of coercive measures, whether sanctions or armed force. Some will worry that taking a case to the Security Council will compromise operational intelligence and make an attack less successful. But any attack that relies crucially on time-sensitive intelligence of this kind is more likely to be justifiable as preemptive, if it is justifiable. Justified preventive action looks further down the time line. What is called for here is an "indictment-arrest warrant," allowing attack when opportune, because the threatener is emerging as a very high likelihood attacker. In the best of circumstances, sanctions or even the indictment itself may signal wide international condemnation of a sort that encourages more conciliatory and less threatening behavior by the threatening state. Indeed, some think this is happening today with North Korea and Iran.

We disagree, however, about the danger of the Security Council's merging the standards of prevention and humanitarian rescue. Naturally, prevention is self-regarding and humanitarian rescue is, or should be, other-regarding. The first is more subject to self-interested abuse. We agree on this. But the standards will overlap. First, because the Charter requires that only threats to "international peace and security" can justify the anticipatory use of force (Article 39) by the Security Council. Humanitarian rescues will thus need to be presented in self-defense clothes to meet Charter standards. So Somalia's warlord-fostered famine became conceptualized as a threat to the security of Kenya supposedly posed by starving Somalis attempting to cross the Kenya border. Even the Genocide Convention delegates enforcement to the Security Council (Article 8) where the Charter then governs the justifiable use of nondefensive force. But more substantively, the legitimacy standards of just war—necessity, proportionality, and noncombatant protection—should apply to both, as discussed above.

We appear to disagree the most when it comes to what should happen if the Security Council should fail to meet its responsibility both to determine a threat to the peace and to authorize a justifiable preventive self-defense. Harold Koh appears to want an unarticulated act of reflexive self-defense that, post facto, the state would try to excuse by reason of necessity, or radical incapacity to act otherwise. Any deliberation about standards beforehand seems to worry him by opening up floodgates of self-delusional, self-interested justification. No one, in my opinion, should be unconcerned about the dangers he articulates, but a blanket prohibition would not be heeded and is not the best antidote. A continuation of the deliberation that brought the case to the Security Council would be preferable.

The best case for unilateral preventive action will be that the Security Council should have acted, according to the precedents it had established. The best reasons will exemplify the standards of likelihood, lethality, legitimacy, and legality that should have informed the case brought to the UN. Necessity and proportionality should continue to rule and, minimizing infringement of legality, should continue to shape policy. When, during the Cuban Missile Crisis, the White House ExComm came to the conclusion that the Security Council would not act, they rightly sought out the Organization of American States' (OAS) endorsement to enhance legitimacy. Even though Article 53 of the Charter precluded regional organizations such as the OAS from authorizing enforcement action, regional support enhanced deliberation and legitimacy. A blockade, such as the "quarantine" against Cuba, was an act of war, an illegal response to a mere threat, but it was wisely chosen in this case as being less dangerous, more proportional, and "less illegal" than an invasion or airstrike, less like "another Pearl Harbor."[3] They continued deliberating and applying standards, even when they were not prepared to abide strictly by the law. They chose the option that was more proportional than either an air strike or an invasion, the other two options considered, and better as they then saw it to merely tolerating the deployment of the missiles or beginning a protracted negotiation that they reasonably assumed would escalate the crisis, erode U.S. credibility in the Cold War standoff over Berlin,[4] and leave Cuba armed with nuclear missiles. We are all better off today that they continued to deliberate, looking for the more legitimate and the less illegal, and presenting their reasoning to the allies and the public in order to elicit support.

I also argue in these lectures that we would be even better off in the future if the decision-makers anticipated that their decisions would be examined by national commissions and Security Council committees, with a view to establishing what was known, and what should and could have been known, and whether the decision in the light of hindsight should be justified.

In the end, constitutional democrats have little to choose in this matter. Many constitutions, the U.S. Constitution among them, require that the executive consult with the legislature before going to war. The U.S. president must defend the country from imminent attacks, but the House of Representatives should be the body to declare war. In practice, in modern times, declaration has reverted to consultation, but nonetheless an argu-

[3] May and Zelikow, *The Kennedy Tapes,* 189.
[4] Ibid., 148.

ment will need to be made that preventive sanctions or war is needed. A reflex response will not serve this constitutional requirement. The best set of arguments before the people's representatives will be that sanctions or war is necessary because the threat is likely, lethal, legitimately weighed, and least undermining of international law.

Harold Koh is correct that talking about standards for acting in the absence of Security Council authorization can undermine the power of the established rules of law. But the states that ratified the UN Charter were not ratifying a suicide pact. Koh acknowledges that the rules will sometimes be broken; the issue remains whether they should be broken only reflexively, instinctively, in order to protect the sanctity of the rules, or instead deliberately, in accordance with standards and with the expectation of review in order to encourage more responsible action.

In conclusion, I am fully aware of the many difficulties raised by the endeavor to develop standards to govern the ethics of defending the nation in advance of deadly harm. But, in the world we live in today, where the nineteenth-century rules do not fit and yet the discretion of leaders is rightly suspect, we as citizens need to propose the standards that our leaders should employ when they claim to protect us. These essays are designed to be a first step in that effort.

CONTRIBUTORS

⌖

MICHAEL W. DOYLE is the Harold Brown Professor of International Affairs, Law and Political Science at Columbia University. His publications include *Ways of War and Peace* (W. W. Norton, 1997); *Empires* (Cornell University Press, 1986); *UN Peacekeeping in Cambodia: UNTAC's Civil Mandate* (Lynne Rienner Publishers, 1995); *Keeping the Peace* (Cambridge University Press, 1997), which he edited with Ian Johnstone and Robert Orr; *Peacemaking and Peacekeeping for the New Century* (Rowman and Littlefield, 1998), edited with Olara Otunnu; *New Thinking in International Relations Theory* (Westview, 1997), edited with John Ikenberry; *Escalation and Intervention: Multilateral Security and Its Alternatives* (Westview Press/United Nations Association, 1986), edited with Arthur Day; *Alternatives to Monetary Disorder* (Council on Foreign Relations/McGraw Hill, 1977), which he wrote with Fred Hirsch and Edward Morse; and *Making War and Building Peace* (Princeton University Press, 2006), a study of UN peacekeeping, written with Nicholas Sambanis. He served as assistant secretary-general and special adviser to UN Secretary-General Kofi Annan, a position in which his responsibilities included strategic planning (including the "Millennium Development Goals"), outreach to the international corporate sector (the "Global Compact"), and relations with Washington. He has recently been named the alternate chair of the Advisory Board of the UN Democracy Fund by Secretary General Ban Ki-moon.

HAROLD HONGJU KOH is dean and Gerard C. and Bernice Latrobe Smith Professor of International Law at Yale Law School, where he has served as the fifteenth dean since 2004. From 1998 to 2001, he served as assistant secretary of state for Democracy, Human Rights and Labor. He served as law clerk to Judge Malcolm Richard Wilkey of the D.C. Circuit, and Justice Harry A. Blackmun of the U.S. Supreme Court. He has written more than eighty articles and authored or coauthored eight books, including *Transnational Legal Problems,* with H. Steiner and D. Vagts (Foundation Press, 1994) and *The National Security Constitution* (Yale University Press, 1990), which won the American Political Science Association's award as the best book on the American presidency.

STEPHEN MACEDO writes and teaches on political theory, ethics, public policy, and law, especially on topics related to liberalism and constitutionalism, democracy and citizenship, diversity and civic education, religion and politics, the family and sexuality, and the political community and globalization. His current projects address immigration and social justice and the impact on domestic democracy of involvement with multilateral institutions. As founding director of Princeton's Program in Law and Public Affairs (1999–2001), he chaired the Princeton Project on Universal Jurisdiction and helped formulate the Princeton Principles on Universal Jurisdiction. He was vice president of the American Political Science Association and the first chair of its Standing Committee on Civic Education and Engagement. With other members of that committee he wrote a monograph, *Democracy at Risk: How Political Choices Undermine Citizen Participation, and What We Can Do about It* (Brookings, 2005). His other books include *Diversity and Distrust: Civic Education in a Multicultural Democracy* (Harvard University Press, 2000); and *Liberal Virtues: Citizenship, Virtue, and Community in Liberal Constitutionalism* (Oxford University Press, 1990). He is coauthor and coeditor of *American Constitutional Interpretation,* with W. F. Murphy, J. E. Fleming, and S. A. Barber (Foundation Press, fourth edition forthcoming). Macedo has taught at Harvard University and at the Maxwell School of Citizenship at Syracuse University.

CONTRIBUTORS

Jeff McMahan, professor of philosophy at Rutgers University, is working on a two-volume study of the ethics of killing. The first volume, *The Ethics of Killing: Problems at the Margins of Life,* which covered such issues as abortion, infanticide, euthanasia, and the killing of nonhuman animals, was published in 2002. He is currently working on the sequel, which will explore the ethics of killing in self-defense, in war, and as a mode of punishment. He is also writing two shorter, more accessible books on war. One, based on the Uehiro Lectures presented in Oxford in the spring of 2006, addresses issues of responsibility and liability in war. The other, based on the Hourani Lectures presented at the University of Buffalo in the fall of 2006, deals with broader issues in the morality of war, including humanitarian intervention and preventive war.

Richard Tuck is the Frank G. Thomson Professor of Government at Harvard University. He is a premier scholar of the history of political thought. His works include *Natural Rights Theories* (Cambridge University Press, 1979), *Hobbes* (Oxford University Press, 1989), and *Philosophy and Government, 1572–1651* (Cambridge University Press, 1993). They address a variety of topics including political authority, human rights, natural law, and toleration, and they focus on a number of thinkers, including Hobbes, Grotius, Selden, and Descartes. His current work deals with political thought and international law, and traces the history of thought about international politics from Grotius, Hobbes, Pufendorf, Locke, and Vattel to Kant. He is also engaged in a work on the origins of twentieth-century economic thought.

INDEX

INDEX

Bush, George W. (*continued*)
preventive punishment, 132–33;
on security threats, 4, 4*n*, 95–96,
99, 107–8. *See also* Bush Doctrine
Bush Doctrine, xii, 25–29; characteristics of, xv; dangers of, 26–28,
41; inadequacies of, xvi, 6, 26;
mislabeled as "preemptive," xiv,
3–4, 25; preventive war standards
and, 47; subjective nature of, 26;
and unilateralism, xv

Cambodia, 35
Canada, 11–14
capabilities as indicator of, 55*n*
Caroline case, xvi*n*8, 3*n*2, 11–16,
105, 105*n*7, 154
case studies, 64–96; comparison of,
83*t*; counterterrorism efforts, 85–
88; Cuban missile crisis, 70–78,
108–9, 157–58; Iran, 92–93; Iraq
invasion, 88–92, 109–11; nonstate actors, 93–94; Osirak nuclear reactor strike, 78–84; South
African apartheid, 66–70, 108
Cassius Dio, 121
Castro, Fidel, 73
cease-fire violations, 35, 66, 69
Central Intelligence Agency (CIA),
91
Chayes, Abram, 109
Cheney, Richard (Dick), xiv, 25, 92,
107*n*8
chicken game, 26*n*37
China: in Cold War, 27; and Iran,
5*n*4; and Iraq, 90; and Taiwan,
28, 33*n*52; terrorism in, 21; and
UN Security Council, 18, 31,
33*n*52

choice of means. *See* means,
no choice of
Churchill, Winston, 38
Cicero, 121
civil order, collapse of, 35, 69
clear and present danger, 45
Clinton, Bill, administration of,
85–87
coalitions of the willing, xv,
114–15, 118
Cold War: basis of, 71–72; covert
operations during, 39; Cuban
missile crisis and, 70–78; deterrence during, 20, 24, 27; preventive arguments during, 27, 39;
South African case and, 68;
threats during, 54
colonialism, 39
combatant/noncombatant distinction, 58, 137–38, 140–41,
153
Corfu Channel, 58*n*26
Council of Europe, 94*n*74
cruelty, 123–24
Cuba, 70–78, 108–9, 115, 154,
157–58
Czechoslovakia, 39

Damrosch, Lori, 35
Dar es Salaam, Tanzania, 85–86
decision making: case-by-case, 58;
case studies in, 64–96, 83*t*; on
legality, 59–60; on legitimacy,
57–59; on lethality, 47–48; on
likelihood, 48–56; multilateral,
xviii, 61–62; national process of,
xviii–xix, 62; real-life, inadequate
deliberations in, 108–12, 114,
116–17; standards applied in, 41,

INDEX

Hamas, 22
Hand, Learned, 45
Hezbollah, 5, 22, 28
Hiroshima, 48n8, 74
Hitler, Adolf, 14, 39
Hobbes, Thomas, xxi, 48, 119–21, 123–28, 151–52
humanitarian interventions: interference with supply deliveries in, 35, 69; preventive interventions versus, xix–xx, 104–8; United Nations and, 33, 36, 36n57, 156
Hungary, 39, 77
Hussein, Saddam, 23–24

IAEA. *See* International Atomic Energy Agency
ideal speech situations, 32
imminence of threat: *Caroline* case and, 3n2, 12, 15; probability and, 16; as self-defense criterion, xiv, 3, 7, 55, 154
India, 28
individualized liability, xxiii–xxiv, 136–47
International Atomic Energy Agency (IAEA), 19, 60, 80n54
international commissions, 62n30
International Court of Justice (ICJ), 7
International Criminal Court, 62n31
international forum: skepticism about, xxii, 126; value of, xvii–xix. *See also* multilateral forum
international law: Gentili and founding of, 122; inadequacies of, xv–xvi, 6, 7; nonstate actors

and, 93; skepticism about, xxi–xxii, 123–26; terrorism and, 115; UN Security Council and, 65; and war justification, xiii–xiv, 3. *See also* legality of preventive actions
Iran: and axis of evil, 27n40; nuclear program of, 28, 92; as nuclear threat, 4–5, 5n4, 20, 92–93; Saddam Hussein and, 81; sanctions against, 154, 156; as terrorist refuge, 4
Iran Contra affair, 109
Iraq: and axis of evil, 27n40; and genocide, 35, 69; humanitarian supplies disrupted by, 35, 69; invasion of (2003), xiii, 24n, 44, 88–92, 95, 106, 109–11, 116; Iran and insurgents in, 5; Israeli strike against (1981), 15, 58, 78–84; nuclear weapons program of, 79n; Persian Gulf War (1990), 23–24; sanctions against, 58, 90n70, 92; as terrorist refuge, 4, 22; UN Security Council and, 33
Irish Republican Army (IRA), 18
Islamic radicals, 4n
Israel: Hezbollah and, 28; and necessity defense, xx; and occupation-terrorism connection, 19n22; and Osirak strike, 15, 58, 78–84, 153–54; and Six-Day War (1967), xiv, 16–17, 53–54
Italy, 79n, 119

Japan, 15, 53, 154. *See also* Pearl Harbor
Jerusalem, 47

INDEX

INDEX

Lincoln, Abraham, 29
Louis XIV, 54

Macedonia, 33n52
Mackenzie, W. L., 11, 13
Macmillan, Harold, 78
MacNab, Allan, 11, 13
Mallinson, Sally, 78
Mallinson, Thomas, 78
Mao Tse-tung, 21, 59
McCormack, Tim, 78
McMahan, Jeff, xxii–xxiii, 120, 153
McNamara, Robert, 72–73
means, no choice of, xiv, 3, 8, 12, 154
Mecca, 47
Meeker, Leonard, 76n51
Mexico, 29
military advantage, 57, 75
Milošević, Slobodan, xviii
Miranda warnings, 114
Mitterand, François, 82
Molière, 31
morality, fundamental principles of, xxi, 120
moral liability: awareness and, 141–42; collective, xxii–xxiii, 136; criterion of, 139; individual, xxiii–xxiv, 136–47; luck and, 141–42; preventive war and, 134–46, 153; proportionality and, 146–47; punishment and, 133–34
multilateral forum: decision making in, xviii, 61–62, 104; phony, 114; procedural solutions aided by, 31–33; UN as, 30; value of, 59, 115. *See also* international forum
Musharaff, Pervez, 22

Nagasaki, 48n8, 74, 117
Nairobi, Kenya, 85–86
Namibia, 67
Nasrallah, Sheikh Hassan, 28
Nasser, Gamal Abdel, 17, 53
national commissions, 62, 62n30
National Security Strategy (2002), xii, 25
necessity defense, xx, 37, 37n58, 37n59, 59, 101–2, 125, 137
Negroponte, John, 110n15
Netherlands, 15, 154
new security threats, 17–25; as challenge to traditional standards of preemption, 17–18; preventive war doctrine and, 51; statecraft and, 18–25; UN and, 31
Nicaragua, 7
Nicaragua v. The United States of America, 7
9/11 attacks. *See* September 11, 2001, attacks
Nitze, Paul, 38
noncombatants, 58, 137–38, 140–41, 153
Non-Proliferation Treaty, 59, 92
nonstate actors: and likelihood of war, 56; threat of, 18; and weapons of mass destruction, xiv, 19, 21–22, 21n28, 25, 93–94. *See also* terrorism
norms, establishment of global, 151–52
North Atlantic Treaty Organization (NATO), xviii, 104, 155
North Korea: and axis of evil, 27n40; deliberations concerning, 116; as nuclear threat, 20, 28;

INDEX

time for deliberation. *See* delibera-
tion, no moment for
Tocqueville, Alexis de, 52*n*16
Tojo, Hideki, 39
Tokyo Tribunal, 16, 154
torture, xx, 102–3, 103*n*4
Torture Memo (U.S. Justice Depart-
ment), 102
total war, 136
toxic chemical stockpiles, 19, 20*n*23
Trachtenberg, Marc, 38
Trollope Ploy, 76–77
Truman, Harry S., 38, 117
Tuck, Richard, xiv*n*6, xxi–xxii,
151–52
"Turbulent Frontier," 39
Turkey, 71, 73, 76*n*52, 76–78

unilateralism: conditions permitting,
62, 157; Cuban missile crisis and,
70–78; decision making and,
104–5; illegality of, 30; new security threats and, 20–21; Osirak
strike and, 78–84; prohibition of,
xix–xxi, 100–101, 108, 113–14,
117; self-defense and, 9; United
States and, xv
United Kingdom, 31, 155
United Nations: High-level Panel on
Threats, Challenges and Change,
31, 31*n*, 57*n*24; and humanitarian interventions, 33, 36, 36*n*57,
156; Monitoring, Verification and
Inspection Committee (UN-
MOVIC), 89; Special Commission (UNSCOM), 80*n*54, 81*n*57;
on use of force, xii
United Nations Charter: Article 39,
xii, 30, 38, 44, 69, 100, 154–55,

156; Article 51, 3*n*2, 7, 9, 10, 85;
Article 53, 78, 157; Chapter VII,
3*n*1, 35, 65, 66
United Nations General Assembly:
"Definition of Aggression," 8–9;
The Responsibility to Protect, 69
United Nations Security Council:
authorization of, for use of force,
xii, xvii, 61–62, 126, 154; China
and Russia on, 18; and Cuban
missile crisis, 78; discretion of,
65, 100; diversity of, 31–32; and
domestic versus international
threats, 65–66, 68–69; inadequacies of, xvii–xviii, 33–36, 62; and
Iraq invasion, 88–89, 109–11;
and Kosovo, 115; and Osirak
strike, 15, 82; Permanent Five,
30–32, 65; politics in, 32; preventive measures taken by, 35; procedures of, 30–36, 89*n*68; and al
Qaeda, 87, 88*n*; reporting to, 9,
10, 62, 62*n*31; Resolution (SCR)
1267, 94, 94*n*74; Resolution
(SCR) 1373, 94*n*74; Resolution
(SCR) 1441, 109; Resolution
(SCR) 1540, 19, 93–94; Resolution (SCR) 1673, 19; Resolution
(SCR) 1730, 96*n*74; role of, 65,
89*n*68; Sanctions Committee, 94,
96*n*74; and South Africa, 66–70;
and terrorism, 19, 93–94, 94*n*74;
United States and, 32–33; veto
use in, xviii, 32–34, 33*n*52, 62
United States: and Britain in early
1900s, 52, 52*n*16; and *Caroline*
case, 11–14; and Cuban missile
crisis, 70–78, 108–9, 157–58; exceptionalism of, 29; as hegemonic